Arenas of Comfort in Adolescence:
A Study of Adjustment in Context

Research Monographs in Adolescence
Nancy L. Galambos/Nancy A. Busch-Rossnagel, Editors

Arenas of Comfort in Adolescence:
A *Study of Adjustment in Context*

Kathleen Thiede Call
University of Minnesota

Jeylan T. Mortimer
University of Minnesota

 LAWRENCE ERLBAUM ASSOCIATES, PUBLISHERS
2001   Mahwah, New Jersey   London

Lawrence Erlbaum Associates, Inc., Publishers
10 Industrial Avenue
Mahwah, New Jersey 07430

Library of Congress Cataloging-in-Publication Data

Call, Kathleen Thiede.
  Arenas of comfort in adolescence : a study of adjustment in context /
Kathleen Thiede Call, Jeylan T. Mortimer.
     p.   cm.
  Includes bibliographical references.
  ISBN 0-8058-2786-2 (alk. paper)
  1. Adolescence.   2. Adjustment (Psychology) in adolescence.
3. Stress in adolescence.   I. Mortimer, Jeylan T., 1943–   . II. Title.
  HQ796.C313 200
  305.235—dc21   00-057678
                                                                          CIP

Books published by Lawrence Erlbaum Associates are printed on acid-free paper,
and their bindings are chosen for strength and durability.

Printed in the United States of America
10 9 8 7 6 5 4 3 2 1

Dedication

In memory of Roberta G. Simmons,
whose work inspired this research.

Contents

Preface

Adolescence is a time when the social world expands—a time of increasing engagement beyond the family sphere to the school, the peer group, and, for most young people in the United States, the workplace. These contexts may present experiences that differ greatly in their tone and content. Some of these domains present problems, taxing the youth's resources. Others promote good feelings, a positive sense of self, and satisfaction. Although people in their everyday lives move across multiple domains, encountering significant others and potentially formative experiences in each one, rarely does the literature in this area take an ecological perspective. This book examines how the constellation of stressors and rewards, in various life domains, influences adolescent adjustment.

An *arena of comfort*, as formulated by Simmons and colleagues (Simmons & Blyth, 1987; Simmons, Burgeson, Carlton-Ford, & Blyth, 1987), provides a context for individuals to relax and rejuvenate so that potentially stressful changes and experiences in another arena can be endured or mastered. It is a soothing and accepting context or relationship that allows people to feel at ease and let down their guard. The arena of comfort thus provides a safe haven; if a person has an experience that is harmful or threatening to the self-image in one context, the injury can be soothed, or compensated for, in another domain through the strong, positive relationships and enhancing experiences that are encountered there.

The concept of an arena of comfort as a protective mechanism directs attention to the multifaceted contexts of adolescent life and their interrelations, which influence resilience. In contrast to the predominant approach in the stress literature that focuses on the number and intensity of stressors experienced by the individual, the arena of comfort construct directs attention to the location of stressors and sources of comfort in the life ecology. It also encourages interest in the adolescent's active role in the developmental process, as young people seek out and alternate between contexts that provide challenge and those that provide solace. By providing social support, a comfort arena strengthens the young person to deal with challenges in other life spheres.

In this book, we use data from the Youth Development Study's representative panel of 1,000 adolescents to address key questions derived from the arena of comfort thesis. In which arenas of their lives do adolescents typically find comfort? Does the experience of comfort differ by gender, socioeconomic level, and other dimensions of social background? Do sources of comfort change as the adolescent moves through high school? Do adolescents typically find comfort in just one or two or in several arenas? Where are they most likely to experience this positive, comfortable state? Are adolescents who find comfort in a greater number of arenas better off—in terms of their mental health and achievement—than those who are comfortable in fewer contexts? Are some arenas more consequential for adolescent adjustment than others? Can an arena of comfort, in fact, buffer the effects of stressful experiences in another context? Specifically, when the home is not an arena of comfort—when family life is fraught with discord—where do adolescents turn? Can comfortable relationships and experiences in the school, peer, and work settings buffer change and discomfort in the family?

Empirical assessment of the arena of comfort has the potential to illuminate key problems and issues in sociology, social psychology, and developmental psychology. It addresses the need to examine the contexts within which individual development occurs and the impact of interrelationships between life contexts on human development. Our consideration of the importance of balancing comforting and challenging contexts indicates that all contexts cannot, and should not, be oriented to maximizing comfort. There are clear developmental benefits in being exposed to challenges and demands that evoke high levels of engagement, problem solving, and the acquisition of coping skills. However, as Simmons (in press) recognized, contexts that provide these experiences must be offset by those offering solace and support.

These notions, in tandem, suggest that the *ecology of comfort*—the distribution of contexts that enable rejuvenation and renewal, and those that elicit distress—may be manipulable, subject to social intervention and to the adolescent's own agency in choosing arenas that encourage growth and provide comfort. Although interventions are often focused on changing adolescents, as when therapy, counseling, or special classes are offered, the results of this research indicate that making adolescents' contexts more supportive and comfortable will be reflected in improved mental health and achievement. Effective interventions could be targeted toward enhancing adolescents' acceptance and affirmation by others and toward providing young people with tasks that yield a sense of accomplishment and success. Consistent with Lerner's *developmental contextualism*, interventions must focus on "the developmental system in which people are embedded" (Lerner, Ostrom, & Freel, 1997).

This book is of interest to sociologists, social psychologists, and developmental psychologists in academic and applied settings, as well as general audiences interested in social support, stress and coping, adolescent adjustment, and mental health.

ACKNOWLEDGMENTS

Support for this research was provided by a grant to Jeylan Mortimer from the National Institute of Mental Health (MH42843), "Work Experience and Mental Health: A Panel Study of Youth." Her work on this volume was completed while she was a Fellow at the Center for Advanced Study in the Behavioral Sciences. Jeylan Mortimer's work at the Center was supported by the William T. Grant Foundation (Grant #95167795) and by the Hewlett Foundation. The Center has contributed to the development of this work in another very significant way. Roberta Simmons elaborated her theory of comfort and wrote the essay that inspired this research while she also was in residence at the Center. The authors thank their editors at Lawrence Erlbaum Associates: Judith Amsel, Nancy Busch-Rossnagel, and Nancy Galambos. The authors gratefully acknowledge the capable assistance of Carolyn Harley, who helped with many of this manuscript's finishing touches. Kathleen Thiede Call is forever grateful to the members of her comfort arena: partner, Greg, and children, John and Emma, who were endless sources of support and positive distraction throughout the preparation of this manuscript. For their encouragement, inspiration, and support, Jeylan Mortimer thanks her key sources of comfort: Roselle, Kent, and Jeff.

CHAPTER ONE

Arenas of Comfort
and Adolescent Stress

It is a truism in developmental psychology that not all people who encounter stressful or straining experiences in life suffer the same debilitating consequences. The dynamics through which psychological resources, coping mechanisms, and social supports can moderate the effects of negative life events and chronic strain have been subject to a great deal of scrutiny. Although people in their everyday lives move across multiple domains, encountering significant others and potentially formative experiences in each one, rarely does the literature in this area take an ecological perspective (Bronfenbrenner, 1979). Adolescence is a time when the social world expands—a time of increasing engagement beyond the family sphere. Adolescent activities extend to the school, the peer group, and, for most young people in the United States, the workplace. These contexts may present experiences that differ greatly in their tone and content. Some of these domains present problems, taxing the youth's resources. Others promote good feelings, a positive sense of self, and satisfaction. This book examines how the constellation of stressors and rewards, experienced across various life domains, influence adolescent adjustment.

ORIGINS AND MEANING OF AN ARENA OF COMFORT

More than a decade ago, Simmons and her colleagues (Simmons & Blyth, 1987; Simmons, Burgeson, Carlton-Ford, & Blyth, 1987) put forward the concept of the *arena of comfort* to facilitate understanding of the multifaceted character of experiences across life domains, as well as their per-

1

sonal consequences. Simmons et al. (1987; Simmons & Blyth, 1987; Simmons et al., 1987) initially formulated this concept as they studied the transition from childhood to middle adolescence. Because they were primarily concerned with changes in the educational setting and young people's readiness to adapt to them, they examined the timing of school transitions in relation to the child's age, gender, and pubertal development. To them, the key outcomes of interest were the child's developing self-image and behavioral adjustment. Like many investigators before them, Simmons and colleagues (Simmons & Blyth, 1987; Simmons et al., 1987) found that, in their panel of White, urban (Milwaukee) youth, life changes did not always have negative consequences. Rather, negative consequences occurred for some adolescents, under some circumstances; others came through the transition to middle adolescence relatively unscathed.

Two hypotheses facilitated the interpretation of their findings; one directs attention to the timing of change, the other to the co-occurrence of discrete changes. First, according to the *developmental readiness hypothesis* (Peskin & Livson, 1972; Petersen & Taylor, 1980), children can be pushed into a succeeding developmental period too early, before they are cognitively and emotionally ready for the transition. In this situation, a host of negative psychological and behavioral outcomes are likely to ensue. The second, the *focal theory of change hypothesis* (Coleman, 1974), posited that it is easier to deal with one life change at a time rather than several simultaneously. Taken together, if change comes too early or too suddenly, at a time when persons are not ready, and especially if change occurs in too many different areas of life concurrently, then adolescents experience great discomfort.

Simmons and Blyth's theoretical contribution was to infer a set of dynamic processes underlying these two seminal hypotheses that pointed to the significance of an *arena of comfort*. In doing so, they highlighted the importance of the particular locations in the life space in which change, stress, and comfort are experienced. Simmons and Blyth (1987) surmised that in periods of life change "there needs to be some arena of life or some set of role-relationships with which the individual can feel relaxed and comfortable, to which he or she can withdraw and become reinvigorated" (p. 352). If at least one context, or set of role-relationships, remains stable and evokes a positive emotional tone, the individual is protected. Self-esteem is thus preserved and behavioral coping enhanced.

An arena of comfort provides a context for the individual to relax and rejuvenate so that potentially stressful changes and experiences in another arena can be endured or mastered. It is a soothing and accepting context or relationship that allows individuals to relax, feel at ease with themselves, and let down their guard (Simmons, in press; Simmons et al.,

1987). The arena of comfort thus provides a safe haven; if a person has an experience that is harmful or threatening to the self-image in one context, the injury can be soothed, or compensated for, in another domain, through the strong positive relationships and enhancing experiences that are encountered there.

Simmons (in press) elaborated the experience of comfort as a self-emotion. *Self-comfort* is described as a balanced state in which the individual feels a sense of familiarity with the self and a high degree of fit with the environment. Accordingly, comfort occurs when the individual is at ease— when arousal is neither very high (i.e., an anxious, excited, or exhilarated state) nor very low (i.e., a bored or depressed state). A comfort arena is a context or role-relationship that "provides a warm, non-judgmental social environment, where acceptance is unconditional. Here is where one feels 'at home,' where one feels at peace with oneself, where one can 'let one's hair down'" (Simmons, in press). Thus, a comfort arena provides experiences of both self-acceptance and perceived acceptance by others.

Although the level of comfort experienced in one arena is important, individuals are involved in multiple roles and arenas. Following the work of Thoits (1983) and Linville (1985), Simmons and Blyth (1987) hypothesized that people who are experiencing change have better mental health and use more effective coping strategies if they are involved in multiple roles. Simmons (in press) qualified this insight by noting that multiple contexts of activity are most beneficial to the person if the same role-partners are not found across diverse life arenas, and if change does not occur simultaneously in many different contexts.

The first qualification addresses issues of network embeddedness and role segregation (Simmons, in press). When roles are segregated (Merton, 1968), the individual's behaviors and identities are invisible to role-partners from one context to the next. If the person has the same role-partners (network-embeddedness) in several life arenas, the freedom to try on different identities, explore, and sometimes fail may be constrained. Failure witnessed by a role-partner in one context may impact on other contexts that the individual and role-partner share; such overlap has the potential to be detrimental if the role-partner assumes that failure in one setting will carry over into other arenas (Stryker, 1980; Thoits, 1983). Punishments and other negative sanctions could also extend from one to the other sphere. (In contrast, this situation could be comforting if the role-partner responds with reassurance and support.)

Simmons (in press) posited that having separate audiences in each context is especially beneficial during adolescence, as the young person begins to experiment with new roles and identities. Although this is certainly not always the case, family members may be viewed as especially constraining at this stage, given that familial expectations for behavior are based on long-term experiences. Parents and siblings have knowledge about the individual's shortcomings and failures, as well as successes, and expectations, built up over a number of years, regarding the former essentially dependent and emotionally immature child. Adolescents may feel freer to act like their current selves among their friends and may shield their parents from their new "on-stage" identities (Simmons, in press). Furthermore, behavior accepted and admired by peers, such as alcohol and other substance use (Maggs, 1997), may be misunderstood or disapproved by parents (Csikszentmihalyi & Larson, 1984).

CUMULATION OR LOCATION OF STRESSORS?

Hetherington (1989) and Rutter (1979, 1985) observed that the effects of stressors or risk factors are cumulative, such that the accumulation of several stressors or other risk factors increases the probability of negative outcomes (see also Masten & Coatsworth, 1995). Simmons, Burgeson, and Reef (1988) linked lower self-esteem, more problem behavior, and reduced achievement to the number of transitions experienced by teenagers (e.g., family disruption, school changes, geographical mobility, etc.). The life events and risk literatures generally emphasize the number and pacing of risks. That is, the greater the number of stressors experienced and the closer they occur in time, the more difficult it is for the individual to adapt (e.g., having one's parents begin the process of separation and divorce, moving to a new neighborhood, and transferring to a new school simultaneously, rather than experiencing the occurrence of only one of these events in isolation or at least having the events occur separately over a period of time).

Simmons and her colleagues (Simmons & Blyth, 1987; Simmons et al., 1987) contributed to the stress literature by extending the paradigm of causation beyond the cumulation of stressors or risks. What is crucial for them is to understand the contexts in which changes and concomitant stressors occur and their location in the total life space, not simply the number of experienced stressors or even their intensity. They argued "that it is not simply the addition of separate stressors that causes difficulty, but rather that it becomes more difficult to deal with a particular change when one is experiencing change in other key aspects of one's life" (Simmons et al., 1987, p. 1230).

Simmons and her colleagues (Simmons & Blyth, 1987; Simmons et al., 1987) thus highlighted the contexts or role locations that are stressful or undergoing change and risky events concurrently. Stressful events occurring at the same time in numerous contexts in which the individual is involved will be more detrimental to adjustment than several changes occurring in one or two isolated arenas. For example, when parents separate or divorce, the adolescent typically experiences a multitude of simultaneous changes in different settings. In addition to the loss of daily contact with one parent, the teenager often moves to a new neighborhood with the custodial parent. Such geographic mobility likely entails a school transfer and a loss of daily contact with close friends. Simmons expected this set of circumstances to be more harmful than if a series of risks were to cumulate in only one sphere—for example, if the parents separate, the custodial parent takes an evening job and another adult (grandmother, cohabiting partner, or stepparent) enters the household.

Simmons and Blyth (1987) hypothesized that some interpersonal contexts are more important than others to the individual's self-image and self-comfort. The level of commitment or involvement may be an important determinant of the relative discomfort associated with change or discomfort in a context. Change or strained relationships within an arena that has little importance may not be perceived as discomforting or have negative consequences for adjustment. Coping with changes in an arena to which one has greater commitment is expected to be more consequential (Stryker, 1980; Thoits, 1983).

COMFORT ARENA CONSTRUCT

Simmons' (in press) formulation of comfort encompassed both micro- and macrolevels of analysis. In general, "the larger social structure and cultural values affect the nature of one's more proximate interpersonal relationships and these interpersonal relationships influence the self-picture and the associated level of comfort or discomfort." For example, the prevalence of geographic mobility, divorce rates, and the stability of the economic environment at the societal level affect the extent to which the individual's immediate contexts are stable or changing, affecting the person's experience of comfort. Conceptually, then, comfort can be thought of as a psychological phenomenon with its source in the social structure.

Although the concept of an arena of comfort was derived from the findings of Simmons and Blyth's (1987) empirical study, it has not been utilized, nor directly tested, in subsequent research. Key insights associated with Simmons' concept of an arena of comfort could be especially fruitful in promoting greater understanding of adolescent adjustment.

First, the assertion that comfort is susceptible to societal forces implies that the levels and distribution of comfort across settings will be different depending on the adolescent's social background or structural location. Second, the implications of involvement in multiple roles for adolescents deserves further attention. Multiple role involvements provide diverse opportunities for social support and for challenging, competence-inducing activities. Change and a certain level of discomfort are widely considered to be promotive of growth and development (Rutter, 1985; Shanahan & Mortimer, 1996; Simmons, in press; Simmons & Blyth, 1987). However, disruption in many spheres of life can become overwhelming. The arena of comfort construct directs attention to contextual sources of comfort that enhance the readiness to cope with, and moderate the effects of, change or discomfort in another sphere. Third, the hypothesis that an arena of comfort buffers the negative effects of change and discomfort, providing a place for the adolescent to step back and recover from stressors in other contexts, could be especially useful in gaining an understanding of adolescent resilience in the face of adversity.

These notions, in tandem, suggest that the *ecology of comfort*—the distribution of contexts that enable rejuvenation and renewal, and those that elicit distress—may be manipulatable, subject to social intervention. They may also be subject to the adolescent's own agency, as young people take an active role in seeking out and alternating between contexts that provide comfort and those that provide stress or challenge.

In this book, we use data from the Youth Development Study's representative panel of 1,000 adolescents to address key questions derived from Simmons and Blyth's arena of comfort thesis. Chapter 3 addresses a series of essentially descriptive issues: In which arenas of their lives do adolescents typically find comfort? Does the experience of comfort differ by gender, socioeconomic level, and other dimensions of social background? Do sources of comfort change as the adolescent moves through high school?

Chapter 4 examines the consequences of experiencing comfort across various life domains: Are adolescents who find comfort in a greater number of arenas better off, in terms of their mental health and achievement, than those who are comfortable in fewer contexts? Are some arenas more consequential for adolescent adjustment than others? Chapter 5 examines the moderating effects of comfort: Can an arena of comfort in one setting, in fact, buffer the effects of change or discomfort in another context?

Before addressing these central issues directly, it is necessary to closely examine processes of stress and coping, risk and resilience. We review prominent hypotheses about why some people come through major stressors relatively unscathed and others succumb to life's difficulties. We examine these hypotheses in relation to the adolescent experience—endemic stressors that place adolescents at special risk for maladjustment and common protective factors that enable them to cope.

A preliminary focus on general processes of stress and coping in adolescence informs our assessment of comfort across multiple spheres of adolescents' lives, their implications for mental health and achievement, and the relative importance of different contexts or role-relationships. Finally, and especially pertinent to Simmons' (in press) predictions about the place of comfort in the stress process, this discussion provides conceptual underpinnings for analysis of the ability of an arena of comfort in one setting to moderate the effects of stress in another.

STRESSORS IN ADOLESCENCE

The impact of stressors in childhood and adolescence is a prominent interest in the field of developmental psychopathology (Compas, 1987; Compas & Hammen, 1996; Masten & Garmezy, 1985). A *stressor* is an environmental condition that has the potential to induce a subjective experience of distress or tension that interferes with normal and more functional patterns of response (Shanahan & Mortimer, 1996; Wheaton, 1990). Whereas event stressors are discrete events, ongoing chronic stressors or *daily hassles* represent lasting strains in the immediate environment (Cohen & Wills, 1985; Compas, Davis, Forsythe, & Wagner, 1986; Delongis, Coyne, Dakof, Folkman, & Lazarus, 1982; Rowlinson & Felner, 1988). Studies of adults (Delongis et al., 1982) and adolescents (Compas, Davis, et al., 1986; Rowlinson & Felner, 1988) suggest that ongoing stressors are associated with adjustment difficulties, and they may be even more detrimental to individual functioning than discrete life events.

Key social stressors for many adolescents are family discord, parental maladaptation (i.e., substance abuse or psychiatric disorder), poverty, unsafe neighborhoods, and living in an area that offers few employment opportunities (Crockett, 1997; Garmezy, 1985; Masten & Garmezy, 1985). Personality dispositions, such as a difficult temperament or self-regulative deficiencies, and hereditary vulnerabilities are additional risk factors (whose influence we cannot account for in this research).

In contemporary discussions of stressful events or circumstances, interest in the absolute features of the stimulus and the necessary adaptive behaviors has given way to an emphasis on the mismatch between what the situation demands and the individual's resources and capacities to deal with it (Eccles, Lord, Roeser, Barber, & Jozefowicz, 1997; Menaghan, 1990). For some young people, ordinary daily experiences and conditions are highly constraining and stressful (e.g., living in poverty, enduring a dysfunctional family, or being subject to persistent racial or gender discrimination). Chronic stressors such as these may be more debilitating to successful adjustment than major negative life events (Delongis et al., 1982; Rowlinson & Felner, 1988). However, some children and adolescents in such difficult circumstances show remarkable resilience and adaptive capacity (Garmezy, 1985; Masten & Coatsworth, 1995; Masten & Garmezy, 1985; Rutter, 1979, 1985).

Adolescence is a period marked by key changes and life events that are often stressful and must be contended with: the onset of puberty, increased autonomy from parents, new relations of intimacy, the transition to secondary schooling, and the need to make career decisions (Eccles et al., 1997; Masten & Braswell, 1991; Simmons & Blyth, 1987; Simmons et al., 1987; Suls, 1989). These transitions require the acquisition of new social roles and identities. The need to make plans for the future that forces adolescents to come to terms with who they are in a manner that is more intense than in earlier periods of the life course (Suls, 1989). The adolescent's growing self-awareness is due, in part, to increased cognitive and perspective-taking capacity (Masten & Braswell, 1991). A high and often stressful level of self-consciousness ensues.

The demands presented by new developmental tasks can undermine the adolescent's feelings of worth and self-efficacy (perceptions of self as causal agent). Self-esteem (the adolescent's positive or negative evaluation of self) tends to decrease during early adolescence (especially for girls), but most youth gradually recover their sense of worth in subsequent years (Simmons, Blyth, Van Cleave, & Bush, 1979; Simmons, Rosenberg, & Rosenberg, 1973). Depressed mood, as well as suicidal behavior and other serious disorders, show a marked increase in occurrence during adolescence (Cicchetti & Toth, 1995; Compas, Connor, & Hinden, 1998; Compas & Hammen, 1996; Ebata, Petersen, & Conger, 1990; Masten & Braswell, 1991).

Gore and Colten (1991) described changes in mental health and adjustment, which become manifest in adolescence, as "developmentally mediated social stresses." That is, distress arises from the very normative changes accompanying the transition from childhood to adolescence. These changes may be experienced quite differently for boys and girls. For example, puberty brings on physical changes that are often unsettling for girls, elevating their self-consciousness (especially for early developers) and altering relationships with male and female friends. In contrast, the bodily changes of puberty are more likely to be perceived as desirable for boys (Bush & Simmons, 1987; Petersen, Sargiani, & Kennedy, 1991). Thus, the experience and outcome of this transition may be very different for girls and boys. Adolescent girls are in some respects more vulnerable than boys, exhibiting increases in depressive symptoms and a diminished sense of mastery (Allgood-Merten, Lewinsohn, & Hops, 1990; Gecas, 1989; Maccoby & Jacklin, 1974; Peterson et al., 1991). Girls, not boys, are at greater risk of depressed mood as they grow older, with this gender difference in risk beginning at age 13 (Ge, Lorenz, Conger, Elder, & Simons, 1994). Although gender differences in depression increase from early to middle adolescence, Compas et al. (1998) found that tests of the interaction of age and gender during this developmental period yield relatively small effects.

Having arguments with parents is one of the most common stressors reported by adolescents on checklists of life events (Gore & Colton, 1991). Such conflict typically concerns minor issues such as household and school responsibilities, fashion tastes, and the hours adolescents keep, rather than their morals and values (Csikszentmihalyi & Larson, 1984). A certain amount of conflict and emotional tension is considered adaptive—an integral part of the process of gaining independence from parents (Csikszentmihalyi & Larson, 1984; Galambos & Ehrenberg, 1997; Smetana, Yau, Restrepo, & Braeges, 1991) and learning to see parents in a more realistic light (Youniss & Smollar, 1985). The majority of adolescents remain close to their parents while gaining behavioral and psychological autonomy (Steinberg, 1990). However, this period of testing boundaries, negotiating greater independence, and learning the skills of self-regulation is often stressful for both parent and adolescent (Eccles et al., 1997; Maccoby, 1983).

Gore and Colton (1991) characterized parent–adolescent conflict as a developmentally mediated stressor. Changes in adolescents' cognitive capacities shape the interpretation and magnitude of these disagreements (Smetana et al., 1991). With greater maturity comes increased awareness of the feelings of others and elevated preoccupation with intimacy and relationships, particularly with respect to peers (Larson & Asmussen, 1991). These changes transform the bases of relationships with parents and friends, upsetting the rules governing performance in both domains (Larson & Asmussen, 1991). At least in the short run, these changes can be stressful and uncomfortable.

Girls appear to be more vulnerable than boys to relational difficulties because their emotions are thought to be more social or interpersonally oriented (Gilligan, 1982). Girls become even more interpersonally sensitive as they move through adolescence (Richards & Larson, 1989). Because girls appear to be more dependent on others for their self-image and self-esteem, they tend to be more reactive than boys to the ups and downs that characterize adolescents' relationships with friends and parents (Douvan & Adelson, 1966). Adolescent boys' emotions are more activity and achievement based (Gilligan, 1982), and therefore less susceptible to the actions and evaluations of parents and friends (Larson &

Asmussen, 1991; Richards & Larson, 1989). These effects persist into adulthood, as the literature consistently indicates that negative social relationships lead adult women to experience greater psychological distress than men (Henderson, Byrne, Duncan-Jones, Scott, & Adcock, 1980; Schuster, Kessler, & Aseltine, 1990).

However, it is not necessarily the case that girls are generally, or in all respects, more sensitive to the stressors of adolescence than are boys (Dornbusch, Mont-Reynaud, Ritter, Chen, & Steinberg, 1991; Menaghan, 1990). That is, girls are more likely to internalize problems, resulting in increased depressed mood and decreases in self-esteem and a sense of control over their situations. However, when attention turns to behavioral indicators of adjustment or acting out, adolescent boys exhibit more problems (Menaghan, 1990; Petersen, Leffert, Graham, Alwin, & Ding, 1997; Simmons & Blyth, 1987; Werner, 1987).

Thus, aging and normal developmental transitions alone create disturbances in the way adolescents view themselves, their relationships, and the world. Relations with parents remain important to facilitating and maintaining healthy development. For many adolescents, relationships with parents may still be perceived as accepting and comfortable. Adolescents who are close to their parents are in many ways advantaged, scoring higher on measures of self-reliance and autonomy (Steinberg & Silverberg, 1986), school performance, well-being and self-esteem (Maccoby & Martin, 1983), and health (Noack & Kracke, 1997). In comparison to peers who are more distant from their parents, they engage in less problem behavior and manifest less depressed mood.

Although the family arena is highly consequential to adolescent adjustment, as young people move into adolescence they spend less time at home and increase the amount of time spent with friends (Csikszentmihalyi & Larson, 1984). The peer group is the one domain that adolescents can more freely choose. They choose who they spend time with and how that time is spent (Hartup, 1983). Because of their discretionary character, we might expect that relationships with friends would be perceived as very comfortable. However, relatively little is known about the character of adolescent friendship and its consequences for development (Savin-Williams & Berndt, 1990).

In addition to experiencing these nearly universal normative changes and accompanying discomforts, many adolescents endure special events and circumstances that potentially compromise their psychological health and adjustment. Marital dissolution of parents is a case in point; this assumes a central place in our empirical assessment of stressors in the family context. Marital separation and divorce are associated with a range of poor outcomes for adolescents, including depression, behavior problems, and failure in school (Emery, 1988; Hetherington, 1989). Evidence from longitudinal studies of divorce suggests that most children eventually do well, but may experience an initial period of difficulty lasting between 1 and 2 years (Hetherington, 1989). Problems of adjustment often precede the divorce (Emery & Kitzmann, 1995). There is considerable evidence that it is the conflict (a chronic stressor) preceding and leading up to the divorce or separation that most adversely affects children's adjustment (Demo & Acock, 1988; Peterson & Zill, 1986), not the termination of the parents' union.

Divorce may set off a chain of events that, combined, have dire consequences for adolescent adjustment. The custodial parent and children often experience severe loss in income and standard of living following a divorce. It may be necessary for the custodial parent to join the workforce or increase the number of hours per week at work. The repercussions of these changes depend on the parent's attitude and what is communicated to children. Financial difficulties may result in a move to a new household, which, in turn, often disrupts children's schooling and peer supports. Such disruption can result in disengagement from school and poor behavioral and psychological adjustment if mixing in and establishing friendships in the new neighborhood or school are problematic (Entwisle, 1990).

As is true for other stressors, not all children in the family are equally vulnerable to the experience of divorce because the nature and level of stressors to which they are exposed varies by gender and age (Rutter, 1990). We are especially attuned in this research to gender differences. Although earlier research suggested that adolescent girls are more vulnerable than boys when their parents divorce (Hetherington, 1989; Hetherington, Cox, & Cox, 1985), more recent studies find few gender differences (Emery & Kitzmann, 1995).

Economic disadvantage and racial discrimination are chronic adversities that increase children's vulnerability (Crockett, 1997; Kessler & Neighbors, 1986; Robins, 1966; Rutter, 1979; Werner & Smith, 1982). Poor and minority youth typically grow up in a world with a great deal of disadvantage and limited opportunities for escape (Nettles & Pleck, 1996). Families at lower levels of the stratification structure also tend to be exposed to a greater number of stressful life events (Baldwin, Baldwin, & Cole, 1990; McLeod & Kessler, 1990) and have fewer resources to draw on in coping with them (McLoyd, 1990; Menaghan, 1990; Mirowsky & Ross, 1980).

As in the case of marital dissolution, to fully understand the consequences of economic hardship, it is necessary to assess the numerous related circumstances that impinge directly on the adolescent. Parenting styles appear to be key intervening variables (Dornbusch, Ritter, Leiderman, Roberts, & Fraleigh, 1987; Gecas, 1979). Most prominently, Elder and his colleagues' (Elder, Caspi, & Van Nguyen, 1986; Elder, Van Nguyen, & Caspi, 1985) studies of the Great Depression showed that financial loss did not directly affect children in a simple manner; father's behavior, in response to economic loss, emerged as the critical determinant of children's adjustment. It is not hard to imagine that worries over basic needs of food and shelter would leave less time and energy for effective parenting. Children were more likely to suffer if fathers became more punitive, arbitrary, and explosive under financial pressure (Elder et al., 1986). Thus, stress experienced by the parents changed parenting practices, resulting in distress and behavior problems in children (Elder et al., 1985, 1986; Lempers, Clark-Lempers, & Simons, 1989; McLoyd, 1990).

ADOLESCENT RESILIENCE, PROTECTIVE FACTORS, AND COPING

Growing recognition that young people raised in adverse conditions often grow up to be well-functioning and competent adults (Garmezy, 1985; Rutter, 1979) has heightened interest in resilience and protective factors (Masten & Coatsworth, 1995; Masten & Garmezy, 1985; Rutter, 1985). Garmezy's (1985) triad of protective factors is especially prominent: (a) resources deriving from the personality dispositions of the child; (b) a warm, emotionally supportive family environment; and (c) the presence of extended support systems to the family. Masten and Braswell (1991) expanded on this triad, outlining the following factors that enhance coping: (a) dispositional resiliency to stress (e.g., easy temperament); (b) cognitive or problem-solving abilities; (c) a close relationship with an effective adult parent, role model, or mentor; (d) socioeconomic advantage; and (e) the quality of the school environment.

Lazarus and Folkman (1984) described *coping* as the process of managing external or internal demands that the person views as difficult and exceeding available resources. Thus, it is a response to a condition or situation rather than an enduring property of the individual (Hauser & Bowlds, 1990). Following from this conceptualization, *coping* refers to behavior or emotional activity, what an individual does to handle a stressful situation. Some stressors are clearly beyond the adolescent's control and must be accommodated or adapted to rather than overcome (e.g., parental divorce or family economic disadvantage).

Although attempts to escape difficult situations sometimes result from ineffective coping, there are benefits to distancing the self from unalterably bad situations (Hetherington, 1989; Rutter, 1985, 1990). For example, Elliott and Voss (1974) examined the relationship between delinquency and school dropout. They found that for many students, feelings of failure and association with delinquent peers in the school context are mutually reinforcing and conducive to delinquent behavior. Elliott and Voss (1974) explained that school can be a frustrating experience from which the youth may attempt to escape. In their study, rebellious behavior was often exhibited through delinquent behavior in and outside school. Having escaped the discomfort experienced in school and the exposure to delinquent peers, the rate of delinquency and contact with police declined once the student dropped out. Thus, escaping the frustrations and influences of school resulted in rather immediate improvements in boys' behavioral adjustment, but in the long term, dropping out clearly has negative consequences.

In addition to features of the social environment (e.g., availability of a support), aspects of the self (e.g., self-esteem and self-efficacy) are resources for coping and resilience in the face of life stressors (Compas, 1987). Self-worth and confidence in the ability to take control over one's circumstances and to meet life's challenges are key correlates of resiliency (Brown, Eicher, & Pertie, 1986; Rutter, 1985, 1990; Silbereisen & Walper, 1988; Werner, 1987). Feeling confident and competent motivates the individual to tackle a problem, persist longer, devote more energy to its resolution (Bandura, 1986), and avoid dysfunctional problem-solving strategies (Nurmi, 1997). Moreover, successful coping with problems reinforces feelings of self-worth and efficacy. Werner and Smith (1982) found that intrapersonal factors (i.e., self-esteem and efficacy) are the most influential protective mechanisms during adolescence, whereas temperament and characteristics of the caregiving environment are of greater importance during infancy and childhood.

In his pursuit of mechanisms that allow the individual to overcome risk, Rutter (1985) asserted that the person's willingness to *encounter* stress, rather than simply react to it, is crucial. Being able to confront a problem and work toward a solution, rather than withdraw from it, is what is meant by *encountering* stress. Such willingness and active engagement is strongly tied to the individual's feelings of self-worth and mastery.

Rutter (1985) pointed out that the process of coping is not necessarily immediately satisfying or beneficial. Rather, successful negotiation of a risk situation or stressful event, even if highly straining at the time, may better prepare the individual for future challenges, thereby promoting resilience (Elder, 1974). Moreover, the process of coping with stressors may foster competence while also being anxiety provoking and disturbing (Masten & Coatsworth, 1995). The process of gradual, controlled exposure to stressors, resulting in enhanced future coping capacity, has been referred to as a *steeling* or an *inoculation* process (Bleuler, 1978; Murphy & Moriarity, 1976; Rutter, 1990). However, stressful experiences, if experienced too soon when the person has inadequate capacity to cope, may sensitize the individual, increasing susceptibility to later stressors. How the individual deals with prior changes and stressors influences subsequent coping ability (Rutter, 1985; Shanahan & Mortimer, 1996; Simmons & Blyth, 1987; Simmons et al., 1987).

Three processes are pertinent to an understanding of contextually based resources for coping. All point to the importance of social support for psychological adjustment in the presence of negative life events (Cauce, Felner, & Primavera, 1982; Compas, Slavin, Wagner, & Vannatta, 1986; Robinson & Garber, 1995). First, direct practical assistance in dealing with a stressor may be available in the environment, provided by other persons or social agencies. Second, perceptions that social support is available can alter the individual's appraisal of the situation and the ability to handle it (Cohen & Wills, 1985). Problems may seem more easily surmountable with the knowledge that supportive others could be called on if needed. Finally, supportive relationships as well as experiences of success in a given environmental arena foster the development of personal resources that, in turn, promote effective coping (Rutter, 1990).

Studies of adults (Pearlin & McCall, 1990; Weiss, 1990) suggest that the most effective forms of support flow from the normal exchange between friends rather than from explicitly soliciting and receiving help. Similarly, as Savin-Williams and Berndt (1990) explained in their review of literature on adolescent friendships,

> Several theorists have claimed that friends rarely give support intentionally to one another; rather support is obtained as a by-product of participating in close relationships. In this view merely having friends and interacting with them give adolescents a sense of belonging and security that increases their mental health. Thus, identifying how friends support one another is equivalent to specifying how close friends behave with one another. (p. 303)

As is the case for adults (Cohen & Wills, 1985; House, Landis, & Umberson, 1988; Kessler & McLeod, 1985), perceptions of support may be central to adolescent coping and mental health.

Social support is of foremost importance to an understanding of intrapersonal sources of resilience; secure and supportive personal relationships strengthen and sustain positive self-concepts and feelings of competence. Given that an individual moves from one set of role-relationships to another, it is important to understand whether persons and experiences in the new arenas reinforce a positive or negative self-image. According to Rutter (1990), "there are many sources of self-esteem and self-efficacy and that a lack in one domain of life may be compensated for by the presence of relevant experiences in another domain" (p. 197).

The school context may offer opportunities and experiences not available in the family setting that strengthen coping skills. Describing his follow-up study of women raised in an institution, Rutter (1990) noted the compensating power of experiences in various contexts. Positive school experiences were particularly important for the ex-care group of women (Quinton, Rutter, & Liddle, 1984). These positive school experiences rarely included high academic achievement, as was the case with a comparison group. Rather, any opportunity to gain competence and build esteem—whether through music, crafts, extracurricular activities, or relationships with faculty members—had a positive influence. Rutter (1990) speculated that the reason the school effect did not hold in the comparison group was that "most of the girls had ample sources of reward in the family, so that the additional experiences of success at school merely reinforced self-esteem, rather than creating it" (p. 197).

Environments provide greater or lesser opportunity to accomplish important tasks, enabling the person to be successful in coping with challenges (Bandura, 1977, 1986; Nurmi, 1993; Rutter, 1990). A broad range of experiences could come into play, including the acquisition of responsibilities, learning new skills, social successes, and academic achievements (Nurmi, 1997). Grades are especially important for adolescents' sense of competence and self-confidence (Eccles et al., 1997). The specific task is less important than the information the individual receives about the self in mastering it.

Effective coping skills thus arise through self-concept formation: Experiences at school (or at work) foster favorable self-attributions, positive reflected appraisals, and advantageous social comparisons (Eccles et al., 1997; Gecas & Seff, 1989). Adolescents see themselves as successful and skilled in accomplishing what they set out to do, in seeing themselves through the eyes of others, and through comparing themselves to their peers. These perceptions heighten self-esteem and mastery (Call, 1996; Call, Mortimer, & Shanahan, 1995; Rosenberg & McCullough, 1981).

In comparison to the broad literatures on development in the family, school, and peer contexts, there is little research concerning how the work environment fosters adolescents' coping skills. The work context offers a new set of role-relationships and responsibilities and a kind of exposure to adults that is different from that experienced at home or in school. The young person may be given the same or similar tasks to those performed by adults in the work setting, fostering a new sense of maturity. Work also creates opportunities to learn skills that may increase feelings of self-worth and mastery. Work must be included in our ecological or multidomain analysis because national surveys (Manning, 1990) show that the majority of adolescents were employed at the time the Youth Development Study began (61% of 10th graders and 90% of 11th and 12th graders). Most employed youth find jobs in the naturally occurring labor market. Thus, their work is separated from other domains of their lives, not connected to family or school.

Part-time work has been found to have direct impacts on adolescent functioning. For example, work conditions that provide opportunities for advancement and good pay enhance adolescents' perceptions of self-competence, whereas work–school conflicts diminish self-efficacy (Finch, Shanahan, Mortimer, & Ryu, 1991). Learning opportunities at work also enhance occupational reward values, which are clearly implicated in career decision making (Mortimer, Pimentel, Ryu, Nash, & Lee, 1996).

The school and work settings may promote the acquisition of positive values and behaviors, provide opportunities for experiences of success and satisfaction, and foster feelings of competence and self-esteem in a manner unavailable in other life contexts. Csikszentmihalyi and Larson (1984) found that adolescents' moods were enthusiastic and engaged during structured activities such as paid work, classwork, and favorite leisure activities (i.e., sports, art, music). These activities, guided by structured systems of rules and constraints, motivated adolescents to decipher the rules, work toward a goal within those regulations, and learn about themselves through this performance. The skills and values cultivated at school and at work may have a long-term impact on adolescents' mental health and adjustment and may initiate changes in the adolescent that carry over into other arenas, altering the life trajectory.

THE ADOLESCENT AS ACTIVE AGENT

The connection between personal and contextual processes is well captured in the preceding discussion. However, the individual's capacity to seek out environments that promote successful or unsuccessful adaptation has not yet been addressed. Moreover, this *agentic* view of the individual has not received sufficient attention in the risk and stress literature. Gecas' (1986) theory of motivation provides a relevant conceptual framework in which to consider adolescent agency.

Gecas (1986) proposed a theory of motivation in which the self-concept is a driving force in the socialization process. Three self-motives are posited: self-esteem, self-efficacy, and authenticity. *Self-esteem* is "the motivation to view oneself favorably and to act in such a way as to maintain (protect) or increase a favorable view of oneself" (p. 138). *Self-efficacy* is seeing oneself as having control over the environment and the circumstances in which one finds oneself. *Authenticity* refers to the motivation to perceive the self as real, meaningful, and significant. Together, these three motivations provide the basis for conceptualizing the individual as an active participant in the socialization process, ". . . shaping and creating his/her world, as well as being affected by it" (p. 136).

Thus, persons are motivated to maximize their self-esteem, self-efficacy, and authenticity (Gecas, 1986) by choosing contexts and situations that allow them to do so. Environments that work against these self-motives are harmful to the self-concept and will be resisted. Accordingly, the person will actively select contexts that create or reinforce positive self-images and will make stronger commitments to identities that fulfill their self-motives.

The move into adolescence allows the youth more choice of associates and social situations and more freedom of movement between multiple contexts (Feldman & Elliott, 1990). In a review of factors contributing to the resilience of children raised in chronic adversity, Rutter (1985) noted that "one good close relationship does much to mitigate the effects of other bad relationships, and lasting rewards and achievements in one arena may go a long way to offset problems in other areas of life" (p. 607; see also Masten & Coatsworth, 1995). Access to contexts outside the family setting may be especially relevant for adolescents who live in poverty or whose family life is uncomfortable. Risk research documents the ability of resilient youth to seek out a wide array of supports and experiences outside the home (Cauce et al., 1982; Furstenberg, 1987; Garmezy, 1985; Rutter, 1985; Werner, 1987). Indeed, the capacity of the adolescent to forge supportive relations with others is a key factor in the development of resilience (Robinson & Garber, 1995).

Although risk and protective factors, as well as coping processes, have been identified in several contexts considered in isolation, there has been little attempt to uncover systematic relationships between contexts and their developmental consequences. Some researchers have begun to explore the interrelations among stressors, social support, and psychological functioning across social contexts (e.g., Lepore, 1992; Pearlin & McCall, 1990; Weiss, 1990). Of great pertinence to Simmons' arena of comfort thesis, we now turn to the implications of being involved in, and circulating among, several contexts during adolescence.

THE CONSEQUENCES OF INVOLVEMENT IN MULTIPLE CONTEXTS

The concept of an arena of comfort builds on the complexity of people's lives, acknowledging that people have multiple identities, occupy many status positions, participate in a range of role-relationships, and move from one context to another on a daily basis. It is plausible to assume that role strain and conflict would normally ensue from multiple and often conflicting role responsibilities and identities (Merton, 1968). However,

Simmons and Blyth (1987) hypothesized that it is healthier to have access to, and to move between, a number of independent contexts and role-relationships and embrace separate self-identities. That is, to the extent that multiple roles are segregated, failure or loss in one role should be buffered by participation in other role-relationships. This hypothesis is supported by the empirical work of Linville (1985), Thoits (1983), and others.

Using an experimental design, Linville found that individuals who cognitively represent themselves in less complex ways experience greater swings in affect and self-appraisal. Self-complexity was measured using a trait-sort method that assessed the number of self-aspects and how distinct these aspects are from each other (the higher the score, the greater the self-complexity). In the first experiment, 59 male undergraduates completed the self-complexity trait-sorting task. Following this, each participant answered a series of affect and self-evaluation items on a computer terminal, describing how they felt "right at the moment."

Once this task was completed, an error message appeared on the screen, at which time the experimenter instructed the participant to complete a third analytic task, "related to certain aspects of intelligence," and left the room. When the experimenter returned, she offered to tell the participants their scores on the analytic task. Bogus feedback was provided to half the participants, placing their performance in the top or bottom 10% of those taking the test.

The experimenter then left again briefly "to complete the check on the error message." On return, she explained that, due to some glitch with the computer, the affect and self-evaluation data had been lost and requested that they complete these tasks again. Linville found that students lower in self-complexity experienced more variability in affect and self-appraisal following the success or failure experience than those with greater self-complexity.

In a second study, after completing the self-complexity task, 31 female undergraduates were asked to complete an affect scale each day over a 2-week period. Those lower in self-complexity experienced greater swings in affect over the 14 days than those with more complex self-representations.

Linville (1985) suggested that self-complexity may be an important moderator of the effects of stressful life events on physical and mental health outcomes, including depression. That is, the more multifaceted a person's view of the self and the more distinct these aspects of the self, the more likely that person will be able to maintain positive feelings about some social roles or relationships. In turn, these positive feelings can act as a buffer against negative happenings or thoughts about other specific aspects of the self. In contrast, the more simple the person's self-representation and the more that aspects of the self are linked, the more extreme the reaction to negative events and the more likely this negativity will spill over to other self-related dimensions.

The application of these findings to the arena of comfort hypothesis is clear. Given that facets of self correspond to the multiple identities and roles that people take on in the various arenas of their lives, those with multiple arenas of involvement will have a more differentiated set of self-representations. To the degree that these representations lack connection to one another, the person can attain a sense of comfort with the self from those spheres where things are going well, wherein at least a minimal sense of comfort and security is achieved. In contrast, if self-representations are few in number or tightly connected with one another, failures and self-abnegations associated with one arena will likely extend to the others.

Thoits (1983) tested and found support for a similar *identity accumulation hypothesis*. Using panel data from a community survey of adults, she found that the greater the number of social identities, the greater the individual's psychological well-being. Thoits (1983) concluded that multiple role configurations are beneficial because the diversity of involvements fosters a sense of purpose and personal worth. Scholars have questioned, however, whether this is always the case. The meaning and value of social roles are of critical importance in conferring a sense of well-being or, alternatively, distress (Burton, 1998; Reitzes & Mutran, 1994; Simon, 1997). If performance expectations and commitments associated with various social identities are in conflict with one another, the strain of meeting competing demands could lead to psychological distress (Bolger, De-Longis, Kessler, & Wethington, 1989; Simmons, in press).

Implicit in the notion of multiple identities and multiple roles is the idea that these roles provide opportunities for supportive relationships and role-partners who send messages to the individual that they are valued and competent. In his review of the social support literature, Lepore (1992) concluded that,

> individuals who have diverse social support resources might be more resilient in the face of negative social interactions than individuals who must rely on few social support resources. If conflict arises within a social network, individuals with limited social support networks may be less able to find help for coping with the social conflict. (p. 859)

The idea that social support from one source can compensate for a lack of support in another context implies that various sources of support are interchangeable. However, some relationships are quite specialized, serving very specific needs, and cannot be substituted (Lepore, 1992; Lowenthal, Thurnher, & Chiriboga, 1975).

Reviews of stress buffering in adult samples indicate that perceptions of support are more important than objectively measured social relationships and exchange transactions. Several investigators (Cohen & Wills, 1985; House et al., 1988; Kessler & McLead, 1985) concluded that the impact of stress on mental health is moderated by perceived support, but not by membership in social networks. It may be inferred that network connections may be maintained even if they are not supportive. A comparison of the impact of received support and perceived support among adults indicates that the perceptions of available support are more critical (Wethington & Kessler, 1986).

Thus, multiple identities or roles should buffer against failure and loss because the individual has other involvements to fall back on. Having multiple roles diminishes the stressful impact of any single role (Kandel, Davies, & Raveis, 1985; Linville, 1985; Thoits, 1983), as Linville (1985) cautioned in her title, "Don't Put All of Your Eggs in One Cognitive Basket."

Gender differences are again of interest because theory and research indicate that adult women encounter more difficulty in managing multiple-role involvements than do men (Hirsch & Rapkin, 1986). We turn now to a discussion of the relationship between contexts that are sources of distress and those that are sources of comfort.

FAMILIAL DISTRESS AND EXTRAFAMILIAL COMFORT

The home is often characterized as a safe haven (Lasch, 1977), a place where the individual finds shelter from the day's events. At various points in this research, we adopt a different perspective. In our examination of the buffering effects of comfort, the family arena is conceptualized as a major context for the experience of stress in adolescence, both acute or eventlike stressors (i.e., the occurrence of a change in the father's employment status, change in family composition, or experiencing a geographic move) and chronic or ongoing stressors (i.e., strained relationships with parents). Again, although a certain amount of tension and friction between adolescents and their parents is normative (Brooks-Gunn, 1991; Smetana et al., 1991), high levels of conflict have deleterious consequences (Galambos & Ehrenberg, 1997).

Parent–adolescent relationships lacking communication and affection have been described as ongoing proximal stressors (Cohen & Wills, 1985; Wheaton, 1990). Uncomfortable or unsupportive relationships with parents have been shown to influence a range of adolescent outcomes, such as problem behavior (Jessor & Jessor, 1977; LeCroy, 1989), the self-concept (Gecas & Seff, 1991; Mortimer, Lorence, & Kumka, 1986), psychological adjustment, academic performance (Maccoby & Martin, 1983), self-reliance, and indicators of responsible independence (Steinberg & Silverberg, 1986). Optimal parenting at this stage enables adolescents to attain autonomy and an identity that is separate from the parents while maintaining connectedness (Galambos & Ehrenberg, 1997). Evidence that problems with parents have negative effects on psychological and behavioral adjustment holds across socioeconomic and racial groups.

When the home is not an arena of comfort—when family life is fraught with discord—where do adolescents turn? There are several potential arenas the adolescent may turn to when family relations are stressful. This book explores the extent to which adolescents receive support from, and have positive experiences in, the arenas of friendship, school, and work. It appears that social support's direct effect on adolescents (Savin-Williams & Berndt, 1990; Windle, 1992), from whatever context, is similar to that of adults, fostering feelings of belonging and well-being that, in turn, enhance effective coping. The greater the social support received or perceived, the better the adolescent's mental health and behavioral adjustment.

Although social support, as well as other positive life experiences, may be expected to have generally positive consequences for personal development (main or additive effects), investigators of stress buffering are most interested in conditional or interactional effects. The buffering effect of social support is demonstrated when the effects of stressors on felt distress, or other negative outcomes, are greatest when support is lacking rather than when support is present.

Studies of stress buffering during adolescence investigate whether social support from family and friends moderates the effects of life events on an assortment of outcomes (Windle, 1992). However, evidence concerning the conditioning effects of social support are not consistent; findings vary depending on characteristics of subjects and the particular measures of support used in a given investigation, such as the number of supportive relationships, satisfaction with support, and the amount of support that is actually received. Mixed findings make it difficult to draw conclusions regarding the differential effects of life events among adolescents who experience greater or lesser social support (Compas, 1987; Windle, 1992).

Whereas evidence for buffering effects is scattered and inconsistent among studies of adolescent samples, perhaps the mixed character of the findings is due to the focus on life events and ongoing stressors, without considering the array of contexts in which they, and the social supports that may counteract them, are experienced. Wheaton (1990) pointed out that investigators are increasingly interested in the context and circumstances surrounding stressful events, emphasizing that stressful life events are contextually bound. Of greatest pertinence to us here, the inconsistency of findings may be at least partially attributable to a lack of attention to the particular contextual locations of both stressor and support processes. Social support may be more effective as a buffer if it derives from an arena that is different from the one that is the source of stress.

Lepore (1992) reported evidence of cross-domain buffering effects. In a sample of college students, support from a close friend moderated the psychological distress associated with frequent conflict with a roommate. Because friends provide salient feedback about the adolescent's evolving identities (Erikson, 1968; Rosenberg, 1979), negative information from one source (the roommate) may be counteracted by the friend.

This evidence suggests that support from a person in one sphere could moderate the effects of discomfort in another. For example, a satisfying relationship with a friend, teacher, supervisor, and/or coworker could lessen deleterious consequences of discomfort in relationships with parents. When relationships with parents are lacking in support and guidance, adolescents seek support from friends (Galambos & Ehrenberg, 1997), whose ability to influence and help them is intensified (Savin-Williams & Berndt, 1990). In general, support from friends promotes adjustment in the presence of stressors in other domains (Parker, Rubin, Price, & DeRosier, 1995). In her 6-year follow-up of a longitudinal study of divorce and remarriage, Hetherington (1989) noted that school and peers played an increasingly important role in the children's adjustment. The greater salience of these extrafamily spheres was in part attributed to the security provided by the structure and predictability of the school environment while the children's home life is in flux. Moreover, involvement with school activities, peers, or a responsive adult outside the family was particularly important for adolescents who had distanced themselves from the family following divorce or remarriage (Hetherington, 1989).

As described earlier, experiences at school and work, and support from adults in these contexts, may enhance coping skills and moderate the effects of discomfort at home. Rutter (1990) spoke of the compensating effects of school experiences for girls raised in an institutional setting, and (Rutter, 1985) the efficacy of one close relationship in moderating the effects of other harmful relationships. However, it should be noted that adolescents' school experiences are different now from when Rutter and his colleagues did their study (Quinton et al., 1984; Rutter & Quinton, 1984). The women in their follow-up study were 7 to 12 years of age in 1964 when the first set of data was collected.

Currently schools are much larger and more heterogeneous (in terms of ethnicity and socioeconomic status [SES]). Although schools provide a wide array of adult role models, schooling is often structured in a way that restricts the formation of close, supportive, and long-term relationships with teachers (Csikszentmihalyi & Larson, 1984; Eccles et al., 1997). Does school offer adolescents the opportunity to establish positive relationships with adults? Do experiences at school strengthen adolescents' coping skills and act as moderators to the adverse effects of strained and uncomfortable relationships with parents?

Compensating processes may likewise occur in the work setting, especially for students who do not find school particularly relevant or comfortable (Elliott & Voss, 1974). Reciprocal influences between work and family contexts are now widely recognized for adults (Bielby, 1992). Much of this research investigates the spillover of stress between work and family domains (Eckenrode & Gore, 1990; Galambos, Sears, Almeida, & Kolaric, 1995). It typically examines how workplace stressors extend to the family and are alleviated by spouse support (Pearlin & McCall, 1990; Weiss, 1990), or how work stress diminishes support from others at home, placing the worker at even greater risk for poor adjustment (Liem & Liem, 1990).

Conversely, Piotrkowski and Crits-Christoph (1981) suggested that, for some women, positive experiences at work (i.e., positive job mood, intrinsic job gratification, job security, and job satisfaction) have salutary effects on their relationships with family members and mood at home. The potential of work experiences and supports to act as moderators of adult family stress has been given little attention. However, some research (Kandel et al., 1985; Wheaton, 1990) indicates that being employed can moderate the effects of marital problems for women.

A recent study by Merriam and Clark (1993) offers interesting evidence of the presence of an arena of comfort. Using a life history-type instrument, they examined the interrelationship between work and love domains. Adult respondents ($N = 405$, primarily female, White, and well educated) were asked to think back over a 20-year period about events and occurrences in work and in love. They were then asked to assess whether the year had been *good, OK,* or *bad* with respect to each life sphere. Three relationships between love and work domains emerged: the parallel pattern, in which the two domains moved together and change in one domain was reflected by change in another; the steady/fluctuating pattern, in which one domain remained steady and assessment of events fluctuated in the other—in this case, change in one domain did not produce change in the other; and the divergent pattern, in which one domain was high and the other low and change in the one domain was independent of, or in opposition to, that observed in the other. For those exhibiting the last pattern, neither the work nor love domain stabilized for long periods of time.

To gain a better understanding of these patterns, the life history data were supplemented by in-depth interviews with 19 participants. For the steady/fluctuating pattern, the interview data revealed that changes in one domain tended to reinforce the supportive nature of the stable domain.

For example, experiencing ups and downs at work may bolster one's perception, and characterization, of the love domain as the supportive and stabilizing force in one's life. In Simmons' terms, the love domain would be the arena of comfort, enabling personal stability in the face of disruptions in the work setting. In addition, the stable context tended to be the domain of greatest investment and personal identification. Merriam and Clark (1993) pointed out that assessments of the stable domain tended to be of an internal reality—perceived as stable and supportive despite external changes.

Interviews with people in the divergent category revealed that change was viewed in a positive light and valued for the associated challenge and personal growth. Events in one domain were characterized as compensating for events and stressors in the other arena. For these individuals, the authors submit that the work domain played the dominant role as an arena of comfort because work was a source of control, success, and security despite external changes.

Most investigations of work and family linkages have been conducted with adult samples. Are adolescents' accomplishments at work and positive relationships with supervisors or coworkers able to diminish or offset strains due to difficulties at home? Does involvement in work, and the satisfaction deriving therefrom, act as a buffer, compensating for the lack of positive feedback provided by parents? Might support and experiences at work distract the adolescent from negative rumination about relationships and events in the family sphere? Alternatively, if work is stressful or uncomfortable for the adolescent, will these experiences potentiate the effects of family discord?

For adults, participating in and circulating among multiple roles is beneficial to mental health because this involvement gives individuals a sense of purpose, worth, and value (Linville, 1985; Thoits, 1983). In this book, chapter 4 examines whether adolescents who find comfort in multiple arenas are better off than those who are comfortable in fewer arenas. There is evidence that, for adults, negative or stressful events and experiences in one arena can be moderated by positive relationships and experiences in other arenas (Kandel et al., 1985; Lepore, 1992; Linville, 1985). Chapter 5 assesses whether comfortable relationships and experiences in the school, peer, and work settings can buffer change and/or discomfort in the family.

CONCLUSION

The concept of an arena of comfort as a protective mechanism directs attention to the multifaceted contexts of adolescent life and their interrelations, which influence individual resilience. In contrast to the predominant approach in the stress literature that focuses on the number and intensity of stressors experienced by the individual, the arena of comfort construct directs attention to the location of stressors and sources of comfort in the life ecology. It also encourages interest in the adolescent's active role in the developmental process through the selection of interpersonal contexts, and the alternation between contexts that provide challenge and those that provide solace. A comfort arena may act as a source of social support or as a coping enhancer if it is protective of the self-concept. By providing social support and increasing coping skills, it strengthens the individual so that challenges in other life spheres can be dealt with.

Empirical assessment of the arena of comfort has the potential to illuminate key problems and issues in sociology, social psychology, and developmental psychopathology. It addresses the need to examine the contexts within which individual development occurs (Crockett, 1997; Gecas & Seff, 1990; Lerner, 1985; Wheaton, 1990), and the impact of interrelationships between life contexts on human development (Bronfenbrenner, 1979; Lepore, 1992). Especially relevant is Bronfenbrenner's concept of *mesosystem*, which focuses on the interrelations between two or more contexts in which the individual participates. The arena of comfort concept, as formulated by Simmons and her colleagues (Simmons & Blyth, 1987; Simmons et al., 1987), assumes that macrosocial structures, related to social class and ethnicity, influence the character of interpersonal contexts, which in turn affect individual adjustment (Elder et al., 1986; House & Mortimer, 1990; Noack & Kracke, 1997; Simmons, in press). Given its location in a particular historical period and relatively short span of time, this research cannot focus directly on the possible structural, organizational, or historical forces at work in producing circumstances that provide a sense of comfort. However, it can address the consequences of these macroforces in its examination of how adolescents' perceptions of comfort differ by gender, SES, race, and other indicators of relative advantage.

This study examines how adolescents cope with stress, provides an opportunity to examine the consequences of both stressful life events and ongoing stressors for individual mental health and adjustment, and, most important, provides an empirical assessment of the buffering capacity of an arena of comfort.

CHAPTER TWO

The Youth Development Study

This chapter describes the Youth Development Study. The first section addresses key features of the panel; the second reviews the measures employed in this research and provides a detailed description of the specification of the central concept, *comfort*. The last section provides an overview of the following chapters, including the key research questions addressed in each.

DATA SOURCE

This research is based on an ongoing longitudinal investigation of youth development that was initiated to examine processes of socialization to work, and the consequences of working, during adolescence. Because the investigators sought to study youth before substantial formal work experience had begun, the study began during the students' first year of high school, when most were 14 or 15 years old. The sample was chosen randomly in the fall of 1987 from a list of enrolled ninth graders in the St. Paul, Minnesota, School District. Of all those invited to participate, consent was obtained from 1,139 parents and adolescents who represented 64% of the eligible invitees. (Eligibility to participate was defined by enrollment in the district at the time of the first wave data collection and by the absence of disabilities, which would prevent the youth from filling out a survey.) Of those who consented, 1,105 adolescents completed surveys in Wave 1 (1988).

The initial sample appears to be representative of the larger population from which it was drawn. The Census (U.S. Bureau of the Census, 1982) reported that 23% of all families with children under age 18 in St. Paul, Minnesota, were headed by females in 1980; similarly, 23% of our adolescent participants lived in single-parent, female-headed homes. The racial–ethnic composition of the sample (67% White, 9% Black, 4% Hispanic, and 13% Asian) is comparable to the racial–ethnic composition of the St. Paul School District as a whole at that time.

The large concentration of Hmong families in the Minneapolis–St. Paul area is also reflected in this study; 9% of enrolled ninth-grade students and 9% of the sample are Hmong students ($N = 105$). Because of the great differences in culture, language, and prior experiences of the Hmong children, and the special methods used in the study of the Hmong, this research focuses on the general (i.e., non-Hmong) sample ($N = 1,000$). (The racial–ethnic composition of the general sample is 73.6% White, 10% Black, 4.6% Hispanic, and 4% Asian.) A comparison of the resources of Hmong and non-Hmong children, in the face of poverty, is presented elsewhere (Call & McNall, 1992).

Although the sample seems representative of the broader population in St. Paul, analysis was undertaken to establish whether the families in the general sample who chose to participate were significantly different from those who chose not to be involved in the study. For example, families from higher socioeconomic groups could be more likely to join the study because they may be more familiar with research in general or more trusting of the school and investigators. Information concerning socioeconomic status (SES) was derived from the 1980 Census (U.S. Bureau of the Census, 1982), reported at the tract level, to characterize the neighborhoods of all eligible families, including those who consented and those who refused to participate ($N = 1,572$). A probit analysis of the decision to participate showed that none of the socioeconomic contextual variables significantly predicted the decision to become a member of the Youth Development Study panel. It was concluded that the sample is quite representative of the general population of public high school students in this school district (Finch et al., 1991; Mortimer, Finch, Shanahan, & Ryu, 1992a).

In this continuing study, questionnaire data were obtained annually through the high school years, and annual data collection is ongoing. This research uses data collected during the first 3 years of the study. Because of our interest in acquiring information from as many youth as possible, the data were obtained in classrooms, by mail (following mailing procedures recommended by Dillman, 1983), and by in-home survey administrations in the presence of a staff member. Questionnaires were completed by 1,000 ninth graders in 1988. By 1990, 954 of the same adolescents completed surveys, yielding a retention rate of 95.4% across the three waves. In the first year of the study, mailed questionnaires were also obtained from 1,573 parents (924 mothers and 649 fathers) of the adolescent participants, who constituted 96% of all mothers and 90% of all fathers who were living with the child. Information pertaining to family SES was obtained directly from the parents.

MEASUREMENT

After a general description of the concept of comfort, we describe how comfort is measured in each of the four arenas of interest: family, school, peer, and work. This is followed by a delineation of measures of change in the family arena, and adolescent mental health and achievement measures. (A detailed list of indicators for all measures used in the study is provided in Appendix A.)

Comfort

Following Simmons (in press), comfort in a context may be indicated by feelings of calmness, satisfaction, acceptance, and ease, as opposed to high arousal, stimulation and challenge, disapproval, and discontent. Simmons (in press) described comfort as a feeling of fit between self and the environment. The degree or intensity of feelings of comfort may vary from day to day, but, in general, comfort is an enduring quality of the person–context interaction. To measure this construct, a respondent might simply be asked about feelings of comfort in a given context. However, given the variety of ways that adolescents might interpret and respond to this common term, this may not be an optimal strategy.

Our indicators of comfort in the family, school, peer, and work contexts assess the level of satisfaction in a particular arena or role-relationship and the positive or negative evaluation of interpersonal and other experiences encountered there. Thus, comfort is indicated by warm, positive, and supportive relationships, as well as by a sense of acceptance, satisfaction, and calmness. Comfort is examined within the family, school, peer group, and work domains.

Consistent with Simmons (in press), we conceptualize comfort as a qualitative state. She posited that having a context that provides unconditional acceptance from others is a prerequisite to mental health. In a comfortable arena, the person does not have to worry about presentation of self. This implies a degree of predictability of the acceptance and support received in that context. If it is to be deemed an arena of comfort, people cannot feel ambiguous about whether they will be accepted, flaws and all, or about the level of satisfaction they experience. To offer respite and protection, the individual must be able to think of the setting as a *sure thing*, providing good relationships and positive experiences that can be counted on.

Simmons did not view the phenomenon of comfort as a matter of degree or as a continuously graded variable. In the interest of coming as close as possible to Simmons' conceptualization of a comfort arena, comfort is indicated by dichotomous variables. Thus, comfort is operationalized as an all-or-none phenomenon, present or absent. Dummy variables were created based on the content of each comfort indicator and its response options. For example, if respondents indicate their supervisor at work is *often* or *always* willing to listen to problems and help find solutions, she or he is considered comfortable (as compared with those who responded *sometimes, rarely,* or *almost never* to this item).

When there are multiple indicators of an aspect of comfort in a given arena (i.e., five items measure the level of stress at work), cutoff points were first established for each item, reflecting the presence (assigned a score of 1) or absence (0) of comfort. The items were then summed to create each arena-specific comfort index or construct, and a cutoff point was again determined to reflect comfort (R. Simmons, personal communication, May 1991). Only those adolescents who describe their contexts in quite positive terms are considered comfortable in a setting. Consideration of the adequacy of subgroup size for performing the analyses informed some decisions regarding index cutoff points (this measurement strategy is described in detail in Appendix B). (Note that analyses reported in chap. 5 use comfort measures based on single, dichotomized indicators separately rather than multiple item constructs as described here.)

Family Comfort. Measures of comfort in the family are derived from Furstenberg's (1981) National Survey of Children; specifically, these evaluations address the quality of the adolescent's relationships with parents or guardians. Questions addressing the adolescent's relationship with mother and father (or male and female guardian) are asked separately. Included are the youth's assessments of the parent–child relationship, such as perceived closeness to parents, openness of communication, and the extent to which the child thinks the parent is available to turn to for support when it is needed. Adolescent comfort in the family setting is also indicated by the amount of time spent with each parent (or guardian) doing enjoyable things.

Thus, comfort in the family refers to adolescents' relationships with their parents. Relationships with siblings and other family members living in the home could also be assessed. However, the parent–adolescent relationship is so critical to mental health and behavioral adjustment that it was given priority in this research.

Adolescents who responded positively to at least four of the five relevant questions referencing a given parent–child relationship are described
as having a comfortable relationship with that parent. Based on this criterion (described more fully in Appendix B), approximately 59% of
10th-grade adolescents report comfortable relationships with their mothers, and 35% report comfort with their fathers. This distribution seems
reasonable because relationships with mothers are typically described as
warmer and more intimate than relationships with fathers (LeCroy, 1989).
Relationships with fathers appear to be more *flat*, and fathers share fewer
activities with their teenage children (Steinberg, 1987).

School Comfort.   The primary measure of comfort in school is the adolescent's assessment of how often their teachers are willing to listen to
their problems and help find solutions. In the school arena, approximately 56% of 10th graders describe their relationships with teachers as
supportive and comfortable; teachers are often or almost always willing to
listen to problems and help find solutions.

We also assess the level of stress experienced in the school arena
through students' reports of time pressures in doing coursework. Reports
of moderate to low time pressures indicate comfort in the school setting
(i.e., the absence of high levels of stress or pressure surrounding the com-
pletion of school work). These measures are adapted from Bachman's
(1970) prior study of school-related experiences, Youth in Transition. The
majority of 10th graders (approximately 66%) report manageable time
pressures with regard to coursework and are described as comfortable.

Peer Comfort.   Comfort in the peer group is indicated by a report
that one has a friend (or friends) to turn to for support and understanding
when things get rough (Ross & Mirowsky, 1987). This measure assesses
whether the adolescent has at least one friend of similar age that can be
counted on for support with some degree of certainty. Here, the term *peer*
implies similarity in age and more freedom of choice in affiliation on the
adolescent's part than is probably true of relationships in the family and
school domains (Savin-Williams & Berndt, 1990). This measure of comfort
with peers emphasizes close, intimate, supportive friendships rather than
the structure and density of links to a *peer group*. Only those adolescents
who report being *very sure* they have friends they "can turn to for support
and understanding" are described as comfortable (approximately 61% in
the 10th grade).

Work Comfort.   With respect to the work arena, measures of comfort
are the most diverse, some referencing social support and others more
task oriented. Work experience measures were obtained from several

prior studies of adolescents and adults, including Bachman's (1970) Youth in Transition Study, Quinn and Staines' (1979) Quality of Employment Survey, Kohn and Schooler's (1974a, 1974b) Study of Occupations, and Mortimer and Lorence's (1979a, 1979b) Michigan Panel Study.

Measures of subjective comfort in the work sphere include the adolescent's perceptions of the availability of supervisory support and support from a best friend at work. Interpersonal sources of comfort in the work setting are not available for approximately 25% of employed 10th graders. This is because some youthwork is typically performed alone, as in babysitting, yard work, or a paper route. In more formal settings, as in a convenience store, there may be no formal supervisor present even when co-workers are present. In the 10th grade, approximately 34% of working adolescents who have a supervisor report feelings of comfort in that relationship. Of those who work in the company of peers, 46% report having a friend at work to whom they feel close.

With respect to more task-oriented indicators of comfort, the work of Csikszentmihalyi and Larson (1984) is most relevant. They found that adolescents' moods were enthusiastic and engaged during structured activities such as paid work, coursework, and favorite leisure activities (i.e., sports, art, music). Activities guided by structured systems of rules and constraints motivated the adolescents to decipher the rules, work toward a goal within those regulations, and learn about themselves through this performance. Some experiences at school and work may allow the adolescents to concentrate on the task at hand, lowering feelings of uncertainty and self-consciousness. These experiences should be comfortable. In addition, successfully performing such tasks boosts adolescents' self-concepts (Bandura 1977, 1986, 1997). Because of their diverse character and/or lack of applicability to all respondents, no attempt was made to form additive indexes of these features of the work arena.

Thus, in addition to the social supports in the work setting from supervisor and coworkers, the presence of comfort at work is assessed by a relatively stress-free work environment, having work that is viewed as interesting, and job satisfaction. The first task-oriented measure of work comfort is an index of work stress (i.e., involving time pressures, having too much to do, being drained of energy, and being exposed to physical discomforts). Jobs that are highly stressful (approximately 23% in the 10th grade) demand high levels of arousal; here they are defined as uncomfortable. At the opposite end of the spectrum, jobs that are perceived as boring (approximately 29%) produce uncomfortably low levels of arousal. Thus, boredom is a second task-related indicator of comfort. The third indicator, satisfaction, is a global evaluation of work experience, indicative of general feelings of comfort (the vast majority of 10th-grade workers, 85%, describe their jobs as satisfying).

Use of the Comfort Measures.   These measures of comfort in each of the arenas take a variety of forms; some are single indicators and some are multiple-item indexes. For example, comfort with friends in the peer arena is measured by a single item; comfort with parents in the family arena is measured by five items assessing feelings of closeness and support with both mother and father; two measures are used to gauge comfort in school (support from teacher and absence of time pressures); and five measures assess comfort at work (support from a supervisor and work friend, and three task-oriented indicators).

In some analyses, the full set of comfort measures is utilized to obtain a most comprehensive rendering of this phenomenon. For example, chapter 3 describes the distribution of all comfort measures in the family, school, peer, and work arenas across 3 years of middle adolescence and provides a highly comprehensive and multifaceted aggregate portrait of the quality of adolescents' lives as they move from the 9th through the 11th grades.

In contrast, other questions addressed in this research are best answered by selecting a single key question to gauge comfort in each of the four domains. Selecting one indicator of comfort per arena simplifies the analysis both conceptually and empirically. For example, the second part of chapter 3 describes the number of arenas that are perceived as comfortable to adolescents. Additionally, in chapter 4, the effect of the number of comfort arenas on adolescent mental health and achievement is assessed (i.e., it examines whether adolescents who circulate among, and are comfortable in, a greater number of arenas are better off than adolescents who are involved and comfortable in fewer contexts).

In analyses that distinguish arenas of comfort by means of a single construct or index, the more interpersonal- or support-oriented measures have been selected to serve as measures of comfort. Practically, this allows consistency in the type of measure representing comfort across arenas. All of the interpersonal measures assess feelings of connection, support, openness, and trust with key actors in a context (i.e., adolescents' evaluations of their relationships with parents, friends, teachers, and a supervisor and/or best friend at work). After all, Simmons (in press) emphasized the importance of significant others who provide concordant feedback, confirm the person's self-image, and support and accept the "backstage" self unconditionally. "If there are no significant others who play the above roles, comfort is likely to be absent."

This study investigates four major spheres of adolescent involvement; however, other contexts and role-relationships are also potentially important. The four measured comfort domains do not constitute an exhaustive list of comfort arenas. Adolescents who do not experience comfort in the peer group, school, work, or with their parents would be characterized in this study as lacking an arena of comfort. It should be recognized, however, that some adolescents may look toward grandparents and other members of the extended family, neighbors, their friends' parents, or adults in the church or community for support and guidance (Spencer, Dornbusch, & Mont-Reynaud, 1990; Wacquant, 1992). In fact, the adolescent's world widens with increasing maturity, providing potential access to a greater variety of adult supports and role models (Feldman & Elliott, 1990). Care is taken to acknowledge this restriction in the interpretation of findings.

Measures of Family Change

As discussed in chapter 1, the family context is the change or stressor context of interest. The family sphere was selected as the arena of change and potential arena of discomfort for two reasons. First, the family is the domain of greatest long-term exposure and commitment for most adolescents. Second, change and discomfort in the family context should be highly consequential (Emery & Kitzmann, 1995; Gecas & Seff, 1991; Hetherington, 1989; Jessor & Jessor, 1977; LeCroy, 1989; Maccoby & Martin, 1983).

Change in the family context, as a source of potentially stressful experience, is reflected in the following three transitions (i.e., event stressors): change in family composition (that may also, but not necessarily, reflect a change in the parents' marital status), change in father's employment status, and a geographical move by the family and/or adolescent. (Change in mother's employment status was also assessed. However, because preliminary analysis indicates that this type of change was not significantly related to any of the measures of adolescent adjustment, nor to adolescents' perceptions of comfort with their mothers, it was not considered further.)

Change in family composition is derived from a question in the adolescent survey, asked yearly, about who the respondents are currently living with (see Appendix A). For example, a change in family composition could reflect a transition from a two-parent intact family to a single-parent situation, or from living with a single parent to a remarriage or blended family arrangement, or the adolescent may move out of the parents' home to live with grandparents, friends, and so on. Although these kinds of alterations in family composition pose quite different potential stressors, involving varying experiences, the number of cases in the study, coupled with the fact that relatively few adolescents experienced any one of these compositional changes, necessitated the construction of an index.

The measure of change in father's employment is based on the adolescent's yearly report of whether the parent is currently working. Current addresses are obtained directly from the adolescents each year, allowing us to track and record geographical moves.

Measures of Mental Health and Achievement

The adjustment outcomes of interest are dimensions of self-image, psychological well-being, and achievement. The measures chosen to reflect mental health are widely utilized in the stress literature. Three reference the self-image: global self-esteem or the sense of worth, self-derogation (both based on the Rosenberg Self-Esteem Scale; Rosenberg, 1965), and mastery or self-efficacy (from the Pearlin Mastery Scale; Pearlin, Menaghan, Lieberman, & Mullan, 1981). Two measures address mood state: dysphoria or depressive affect and the sense of well-being (from the General Well-Being Scale of the Current Health Insurance Study Mental Health Battery; Ware, Johnston, Davies-Avery, & Brook, 1979). Thus, the mental health measures reflect both positive (self-esteem, mastery, well-being) and negative (self-derogation, depressive affect) states.

Because there is controversy about the dimensionality of mental health constructs (e.g., whether self-esteem is better conceptualized and measured as a unidimensional or bidimensional construct; see Owens, 1993, 1994) and reason to expect that the subjective meaning of particular questionnaire items (and therefore the pattern of their associations) would change over time or differ across subgroups, measurement structures were given considerable preliminary attention. For example, if certain indicators of self-esteem were more strongly related to a self-esteem construct for boys than for girls, constructing weighted composite indexes in the same way for each group could be misleading. Moreover, different items might better reflect depressive affect as young people grow older.

The item loadings for each of the mental health and adjustment constructs were therefore derived from a series of confirmatory factor analyses (using LISREL [linear structural relations] VII). Because the study examines adolescent mental health over time, with a particular focus on gender differences, the measurement structure of each mental health construct was assessed by constraining corresponding unstandardized lambda coefficients to be equal across waves and gender. Fully constrained models were then compared to freely estimated models. The analyses reveal that the measurement structures of the mental health constructs are similar across waves and for girls and boys. Therefore, unstandardized lambda coefficients from the fully constrained models are used as item weights. (The full list of indicators and their standardized coefficients are provided in Appendix A.)

Grade point average (GPA) reflects the adequacy of performance in school and is an indicator of behavioral adjustment in adolescence. Because of its importance for college admission and because grades are believed to reflect intellectual ability as well as competence more generally, it tends to have high salience for the student and significant others. GPA is measured by a self-report item included annually in the adolescent survey.

KEY RESEARCH QUESTIONS

The following chapter (chap. 3) attempts to answer a number of questions. First, we asked to what extent do adolescents find comfort in each of the four spheres of involvement—in the family, among friends, at school, and at work? Simmons (in press) asserted that feelings of comfort are responsive to societal forces. Therefore, we examine the relation of comfort to background characteristics that are reflective of structural location and linked to such macroforces. Because of their disadvantage and exposure to discrimination, minorities, the foreign-born, females, adolescents of lower SES, and those from single-parent and other alternative family forms may have fewer arenas of comfort than those in more advantaged circumstances. The distribution of comfort is analyzed for subgroups of adolescents based on race (Whites vs. minorities), nativity (native-born vs. foreign-born), gender, SES, and family composition (i.e., two-parent vs. other family arrangements) at each wave (9th–11th grades).

Another question addressed in chapter 3 is whether sources of comfort change across time as adolescents' interests and activities change. Prior empirical research leads us to anticipate change across time in the particular spheres that are deemed comfortable. For example, adolescence is a period of increased autonomy and independence from parents and growing emphasis on peer friendships (Brown, Dolcini, & Leventhal, 1997; Csikszentmihalyi & Larson, 1984; Savin-Williams & Berndt, 1990). Therefore, we might find that comfort with friends is more prevalent than comfort with parents, with the difference widening over time. The proportions of adolescents reporting high levels of comfort with friends and family are compared at each wave.

Chapter 4 examines whether adolescents who have more arenas of subjective comfort are better off than those who have fewer with respect to academic performance and mental health. We focus on the proportion of comfort arenas, among those that are available to the adolescent, in the 10th and 11th grades. We also assess whether some contexts are more consequential for, or protective of, adolescents' adjustment.

Chapter 5 investigates whether the presence of an arena of comfort moderates (decreases) the effect of change and/or discomfort in another sphere of involvement. As noted earlier, the buffering hypothesis—that comfort in certain contexts conditions the effects of stressful changes in other arenas of life (Simmons & Blyth, 1987; Simmons, Burgeson, Carlton-Ford, & Blyth, 1987)—is key to the very conceptualization of arena of comfort. The capacity of an extrafamilial comfort arena to modify the effects of a variety of changes (event stressors) in the family domain is considered.

Because it is reasonable to suppose that the processes of stress and coping implicated in the arenas of comfort thesis would be different for boys and girls, gender differences are given special attention in examining the key questions. For example, there is evidence that adolescent girls perceive their friendships to be closer and more supportive than adolescent boys (Savin-Williams & Berndt, 1990). Research on adolescent work experience also suggests that there may be gender differences in the experience of comfort in the workplace (Mortimer et al., 1992a, 1992b; Mortimer, Finch, Dennehy, Lee, & Beebe, 1994).

Moreover, the repercussions of change in the family could vary for young males and females. As a case in point, boys may be more affected by a change in fathers' employment status; the change may boost or impede fathers' effectiveness in modeling the breadwinner role for their sons (Elder et al., 1986). Moreover, one gender could be more responsive to certain comfort arenas than the other. Peer support may be more consequential for girls than boys because social affiliations and close friendships are thought to be more important to females than males (Gilligan, 1982). Discomfort with parents may, as a result, be more detrimental to girls than boys (Elder et al., 1986; Hetherington, 1989).

This chapter described the methodology of the study, the source of data to be used, the measurement specification, and the key research questions. The next chapter examines the presence of comfort at home, at school, with friends, and at work for adolescents, as well as the proportion of arenas that adolescents describe as comfortable in the 9th, 10th, and 11th grades of high school.

CHAPTER THREE

The Social Location
of Comfort in Adolescence

In what spheres of their lives do adolescents typically find comfort? Do the sources of comfort change as they grow older? Whereas most prior research examined only one or two settings in isolation, our initial descriptive analysis assesses adolescents' perceptions of supportive, comfortable experiences in four major spheres of their lives—the family, school, peer group, and, for those who are employed, the work setting. In view of what is known about these contexts, what might be anticipated about subjective comfort in each one? How might the perception of comfort differ across key subgroups of the adolescent population? To address this question, we examine differences in experiences of comfort by widely acknowledged indicators of advantage and disadvantage: gender, race, nativity, socioeconomic status (SES), and family composition.

COMFORT WITH PARENTS

Although adolescence is no longer widely thought of as a period of storm and stress, or of great turbulence in the family setting, some tension between parent and adolescent is typical, especially surrounding issues of autonomy (Csikszentmihalyi & Larson, 1984; Galambos & Ehrenberg, 1997; Steinberg, 1990). Ambivalence is endemic in the relationship between parent and adolescent due to the transitional character of this period. Although adolescents generally seek independence from their parents and spend increasing time outside the family with friends, they are still quite dependent on their parents for financial and emotional support.

Parents play a prominent role in adolescents' successful navigation through the developmental changes that accompany adolescence. Discussions with parents tend to concern pragmatic issues, such as the day-to-day organization of the household, vacation or holiday plans, and future goals (Csikszentmihalyi & Larson, 1984). When asked to report the quality of their emotional experience in different settings, adolescents indicate being less self-conscious and better able to concentrate at home, as compared with the more extreme emotional highs and lows reported with friends or at school (Csikszentmihalyi & Larson, 1984). Csikszentmihalyi and Larson (1984) characterized the home as a "balance wheel in the emotional swings of adolescent life" (p. 134). Because emotions while at home may be more moderate overall than those experienced in extrafamilial settings, relations with mothers and fathers are likely to be rated as comfortable.

In general, adolescents perceive their relationships with their mothers to be more intimate and supportive, whereas relationships with fathers are more emotionally flat (LeCroy, 1989; Steinberg, 1987). Although relationships with fathers are usually more distant, LeCroy (1989) found that close attachments to fathers were better predictors of high self-esteem and low rates of problem behavior than closeness with mothers. LeCroy (1989) explained that "since fathers do not generally have intimate attachments to their children, when they do share intimacy it can be particularly salient" (p. 145). Barber and Thomas (1986) found that same-sex parent–child relationships were rated more positively and had a greater impact on adolescent self-esteem than cross-sex relationships. Mother–daughter relationships are the most intense emotionally; father–daughter relationships are the least (Steinberg, 1987).

Family structure also appears to affect the level of perceived comfort. Distant and strained parent–adolescent relationships are reportedly more prevalent within single-parent families and stepfamilies (Emery & Kitzmann, 1995; Steinberg, 1990), whereas relations are closer in intact two-parent families. Close, supportive parent–adolescent relations also become more prevalent as SES increases (Gecas, 1979; Mortimer et al., 1986), which may be linked to a more authoritative (vs. authoritarian) parenting style at higher social class levels (Baumrind, 1987).

Relatively little is known about variations in family relations among minority groups; differences associated with race and ethnicity are rarely separated from those linked to SES (Steinberg, 1990). Immigrant groups tend to encourage interdependence among members in their community (Nidorf, 1985), especially in the extended kin group, sometimes discouraging the adolescent's ties to peers in the host society. However, the pressures entailed in dealing with racial discrimination (Thomas & Hughes, 1986), adjusting to a foreign social system and culture, and/or poverty may undermine parents' ability to be supportive and responsive to adolescents' needs (Baldwin et al., 1990; Lempers et al., 1989; McLoyd, 1990).

COMFORT WITH FRIENDS

Of the four contexts considered here—the family, peer group, school, and workplace—it is in the peer group that adolescents can exercise the greatest degree of discretion over who they are with and the particular types of activities in which they engage. Adolescents exercise some, albeit more limited, control over the selection of companions and activities at school (i.e., which courses to take) and work (i.e., where they apply and to which position). Simmons (in press) pointed out that although persons typically do not exercise choice over all of the arenas they are involved in, when allowed to choose they will gravitate toward contexts that protect their feelings of comfort with self. The highly discretionary character of adolescent friendships would likely enhance adolescents' comfort with friends.

In contrast to childhood friendships based on shared activities, the most important features of adolescent friendships are intimacy, trust, self-disclosure, and mutual support (Bukowski, Newcomb, & Hoza, 1987; Parker et al., 1995; Savin-William & Berndt, 1990). It is with friends that adolescents learn the skills of empathy and taking the role of the other, which foster more accurate self-evaluations as well as better understanding of other people (Rosenberg, 1979; Savin-Williams & Berndt, 1990). Adolescents' choice of friends determines the feedback they receive about who they are (Rosenberg, 1979). Therefore, they tend to select friends who match and reinforce the kind of person they want to be (Erikson, 1968; Kandel, 1978). Time spent with friends is typically spent having fun, participating in leisure activities, talking, or simply "hanging out" (Savin-Williams & Berndt, 1990). Conversations with friends tend to involve lighter topics than discussions with parents, such as leisure activities, relationships, gossip, and, of course, themselves (Csikszentmihalyi & Larson, 1984). Still peers can have a powerful influence on adolescents' academic performance and educational aspirations (Cauce et al., 1982; Coleman, 1961; Entwistle, 1990; Ogbu, 1985).

Girls' relationships with friends appear to be based more strongly on intimacy and disclosure, whereas boys' friendships are characterized as more activity based (Savin-Williams & Berndt, 1990). Girls consistently rate their friendships as closer and more supportive than do boys (Csikszentmihalyi & Larson, 1984; Savin-Williams & Berndt, 1990). It may be that, in general, girls describe all their relationships as more supportive and comfortable than boys because they are thought to be more interpersonally oriented (Gilligan, 1982). However, this communal orientation, which crystallizes during adolescence (Richards & Larson, 1989), may also foster greater sensitivity in girls due to the difficulties in their relationships with peers as well as adults (Douvan & Adelson, 1966).

It has been suggested that minority adolescents or those from lower socioeconomic households may be more comfortable with their friends and more open to their influence than more advantaged and nonminority adolescents (Savin-Williams & Berndt, 1990). If they observe that their parents are without power and prestige, or if family relations are sources of strain, they may become closer to their friends, who come to replace parents as sources of advice and support.

COMFORT IN THE SCHOOL CONTEXT

Feelings of satisfaction and perceptions of support at school largely derive from friendships made in the school setting (Csikszentmihalyi & Larson, 1984; Simmons & Blyth, 1987). It is widely acknowledged that particularly supportive and demanding teachers can change the educational trajectory of their students. However, relatively little empirical work, in comparison to the large literature on peers, has addressed the character of relationships with teachers and their influence on adolescent development. The generally weak ties between students and teachers may be related to the structure of the school as well as adolescents' increased emphasis on peers.

Urban high schools are large and diverse. On one hand, this structure provides a range of adult role models to choose from, thus enhancing the opportunities to form relationships that are congenial to both adolescents and adults. On the other hand, given the large size of each class and movement among many classrooms each day, adolescents' ability to connect with teachers in a meaningful way may be inhibited (Brown, 1990; Csikszentmihalyi & Larson, 1984; Dreeben, 1968; Eccles et al., 1997; Simmons & Blyth, 1987; Simmons, Burgeson, Carlton-Ford, & Blyth, 1987).

In addition to support from teachers, other experiences at school may influence comfort. Large urban schools provide many different kinds of opportunities for the enactment of competence that can foster feelings of self-efficacy and self-esteem. Success in school activities and involvement in an area of interest or activity that is engaging and motivating are thought to enhance personal coping resources (Bandura, 1986, 1997; Csikszentmihalyi & Larson, 1984; Gecas & Seff, 1989; Rosenberg & McCullough, 1981; Rutter, 1990). In contrast, being unable to complete assignments within the constraints of school schedules and deadlines would be a source of strain.

The work of Ogbu (1978, 1989) and others (Felice, 1981; Fine & Rosenberg, 1983; Hendrix, 1980; Valverde, 1987) suggests that minority (especially "involuntary minorities" like African Americans) and financially disadvantaged youth will have less comfortable relationships and experiences at school. These investigators explain that such youth observe the circumstances of their parents and other adults in their neighborhoods, which often provide testimony that effort in school will not pay off. Thus, the lived experience of adult models cultivates a distrust of the educational system and authority figures within the school.

Immigrants to the United States who come to gain political freedom or take advantage of perceived economic opportunities often have different beliefs and values. In contrast to the involuntary minorities, many "voluntary minorities" believe the American ideology about getting ahead through hard work, determination, and education (Ogbu, 1985, 1989). Immigrant students often work diligently on their school work and expect to devote a large amount of time to their studies. Immigrant parents may also encourage deference and obedience to adults (Call & McNall, 1992). The immigrant adolescent's attitudes and behavior may thus evoke positive and supportive responses from teachers, enhancing the potential of the school as an arena of comfort. Given this prior work, we examine whether there are differences in school comfort by nativity status.

COMFORT IN THE WORK CONTEXT

Adolescents increasingly turn their attention and energy toward nonschool activities, including work (Mortimer, Finch, Dennehy, Lee, & Beebe, 1994; Mortimer & Finch, 1996). Nationally, as many as 61% of 10th graders and 90% of 11th and 12th graders are employed during the school year (Manning, 1990). The influence of work on youth development is still a controversial issue, with much concern directed to the opportunity costs of employment. For example, working, and its attendant time requirements, might deprive adolescents of an important "moratorium," free from adultlike responsibilities and pressures (Greenberger & Steinberg, 1986; Steinberg & Cauffman, 1995) to explore interests and identities. Educators fear that adolescents who work may be drawn away from school and have insufficient time to do their homework.

Criticism also extends to the quality of adolescents' experiences in the work environment, given their concentration in the less skilled retail and service jobs. From the standpoint of the adult, *youthwork* may appear to be quite undesirable, involving rather simple tasks and little inherent gratification. However, the same kind of job may be perceived quite differently by the novice worker. Even in so-called menial jobs, the work setting offers the adolescent an opportunity to act responsibly and independently in a role that is highly consequential for adults. In fact, almost all adolescents expect to be employed in adulthood; boys and girls anticipate commensurate levels of involvement in these spheres (Johnson & Mortimer, 2000).

Because the work role is a key component of the adolescent's desired "possible self" (Markus, Cross, & Wurf, 1990), evidence of successful adaptation to employment would likely be a source of considerable gratification. In the workplace, adolescents face new challenges and learn new skills. Experiences of success in this setting can be rewarding and foster coping skills and self-efficacy (Finch et al., 1991).

The level of comfort experienced in a given job will, of course, depend on the work conditions encountered there. As adolescents grow older, they increasingly move from informal work (such as babysitting and yardwork) to formal employment in organizational settings; the tasks they perform also become more complex (Mortimer, Finch, Dennehy, Lee, & Beebe, 1994). Babysitting, which is more common among younger girls, appears to be a quite salutary experience for many (Mortimer et al., 1992a, 1992b). It calls for the adolescent to act responsibly and autonomously and to master household tasks that may be useful in the future. It also constitutes a context in which to care for others—an experience that is often interpersonally rewarding and linked to psychological resilience (Call et al., 1995). The informal work that boys typically perform also requires responsibility and independence (i.e., mowing lawns, delivering papers, or shoveling snow). However, this work is likely to be physically challenging and may not yield the same interpersonal rewards as the informal work performed by girls.

The move into formal work, usually in the service industry, is associated with increased perceptions of stress experienced at work especially for girls (Mortimer et al., 1992a, 1992b). However, despite more frequent reports of stressful work experiences over time, adolescents, especially girls, evaluate their jobs quite favorably in other respects (Mortimer, Finch, Owens, & Shanahan, 1990).

Adolescents from majority and higher socioeconomic backgrounds generally encounter fewer constraints in seeking out new environments (Simmons, in press). Consistently, minority and disadvantaged adolescents are less likely to be employed (Committee on the Health and Safety Implications of Child Labor, 1998; Mortimer, 1994). Thus, part-time employment as an arena of comfort, or of discomfort, will be less available to them due to their constrained access to the employment context. Furthermore, adolescents from more advantaged families may be better prepared to obtain interesting and rewarding jobs. Parents in higher socioeconomic groups may encourage their children to seek out work that provides opportunities to learn independence, responsibility, and new skills (Kohn & Schooler, 1973). In fact, findings from the Youth Development Study indicate that parents at higher socioeconomic levels think that it is appropriate for youth to start working at a younger age than those at lower socioeconomic levels (Phillips & Sandstrom, 1990).

THE NUMBER OF COMFORT ARENAS

Following the work of Linville (1985) and Thoits (1983), Simmons and Blyth (1987) hypothesized that the larger the number of contexts and role-relationships, the better off is the individual. Circulating among a variety of independent relationships and contexts is thought to enhance mental health and encourage the use of more effective coping strategies. Involvement in multiple roles and identities enhances perceptions of personal worth—being acknowledged and *mattering* by persons across a variety of contexts (Rosenberg & McCullough, 1981; Thoits, 1983). Furthermore, involvement in and commitment to several distinct role-relationships offers protection because change or discomfort in any one context can be tempered by relationships and experiences in another (Linville, 1985; Thoits, 1983).

Simmons and colleagues (Simmons & Blyth, 1987; Simmons et al., 1987) hypothesized that everyone needs at least one context that is stable, comfortable, and accepting. Persons who do not have access to any arena of comfort are at greatest risk of poor adjustment. It is not necessarily how much support is actually available or even perceived to be available. Rather it is the perception of the absence of any source of support that is most devastating (Rook, 1992; Thoits, 1985).

We investigate gender differences in the experience of comfort. Gilligan (1982) and others (see e.g., Richards and Larson, 1989) found that girls are more interpersonally oriented than boys and become increasingly so during adolescence. Because girls are more sensitive to relational dynamics, they may devote more effort toward creating and nurturing supportive connections within the contexts they are involved in, and they may be more effective than boys when they attempt to do so. These efforts could yield greater comfort. However, their sensitivity to interpersonal relations could yield discomfort as well.

Adolescents from more advantaged backgrounds (i.e., higher parental SES, nonminority) could likewise perceive comfort across a broader scope of arenas; they may enjoy a degree of status and acceptance by adults and peers across domains that is less readily available to their less advantaged peers. The emphasis on communality and interdependence in some immigrant cultures (Nidorf, 1985) could strengthen the adolescent's sense of comfort in the family realm. Furthermore, immigrant adolescents often perform a prominent role as parents' link to the outside world, which could also strengthen parent–adolescent bonds. The value placed on deference toward authorities and beliefs that hard work will pay off could foster comfort in immigrant children's relationships with other adults in their lives—with teachers and work supervisors. They may also be more likely to find gratification in the noninterpersonal dimensions of their activities. Peer relations, however, may be less comfortable for immigrant adolescents if parents discourage affiliations with nonimmigrant friends or if the adolescent is subject to discrimination and isolation from nonimmigrant peers.

As noted in the previous chapter, data from the Youth Development Study do not pertain to all potential realms of comfort that adolescents may draw on. The survey questions address whether the adolescent is comfortable with parents, whether they have a close friend to turn to in times of trouble, and whether relationships and experiences at school and work are comfortable. Family, peers, school, and work are surely among the most important contexts in an adolescent's life. However, these four contexts do not represent an exhaustive inventory of potential sources of support. Such an inventory would have to include youth clubs (Wacquant, 1992), religious organizations (Cauce et al., 1982; Wallace & Williams, 1997), extended family members (Spencer et al., 1990; Tyszkowa, 1993), adult neighbors, friends' parents, and others. Such alternative sources of support and comfort may be especially important for minority and immigrant adolescents (Cauce et al., 1982; Spencer et al., 1990).

With this limitation in mind, let us now examine adolescent comfort in the four arenas for which information is available, among the total panel and among subgroups of adolescents for whom comfort could possibly be obtained quite differently (i.e., by gender, race, nativity, parental SES, and family composition).

ADOLESCENTS' EXPERIENCE OF COMFORT

The prevalence of comfort across settings is explored using the dichotomous specification delineated in chapter 2 ($1 = comfort$, $0 = discomfort$). Table 3.1 presents the percentages of adolescents, each year, who can be described as comfortable in the family, peer, school, and work contexts.

Change in the prevalence of comfort in a particular setting may reflect a change in feelings about unchanged contexts (e.g., greater involvement in, and excitement about, school activities), change in a single context (e.g., worsening relations with parents), or a shift in the context (e.g., transfer to a new school). A certain amount of contextual change is typical

TABLE 3.1
Percent Indicating Comfort in Four Arenas (Total Panel)

Arena (N = 1,000)	9th Grade		10th Grade		11th Grade	
	Percent	n	Percent	n	Percent	n
Family comfort						
Comfort with mother	57.9	921	59.0	918	59.5	881
Comfort with father	35.4	856	34.8	865	33.9	844
Peer comfort						
Peer support	57.5	921	60.7	853	65.7	944
School comfort						
Teacher support	57.9	993	56.2	949	57.8	892
Low time pressures	68.2	996	65.8	949	61.2	891
Work comfort						
(range of *n* for employed adolescents over						
3-year period = 454–556)						
Supervisor support	41.3	269	34.1	337	35.6	491
Support from coworker	40.3	447	46.0	337	39.1	476
Work satisfaction	84.7	503	85.4	446	87.9	554
Low work stress	89.6	491	86.6	440	83.9	547
Work is interesting	73.8	504	71.0	451	69.3	554

of the adolescent experience (i.e., greater independence from parents, frequent making and breaking of friendships, changing structure of school, and transitory nature of adolescent work). Moreover, apparent shifts in comfort over time in the work setting could be attributable to changing sample composition because not all adolescents are employed at each wave. Only employed adolescents (at the time of each survey) were asked to respond to questions about conditions of, and subjective reactions to, work. Many employed adolescents do not have supervisors; for them, questions about the supportive character of the supervisor–worker relationship are inapplicable. In addition, although panel attrition is limited, data are missing for other reasons (e.g., skipping particular questions). As a result of the varied possible reasons for change, interpretations of shifts across years in adolescents' depictions of relations or experiences as comfortable or not must be accepted with caution. With this cautionary note in mind, because of the inherent interest in change in the sources of comfort over time, we make note of apparent trends in the experience of comfort.

As shown in Table 3.1, more adolescents report feeling comfortable with their mothers than with their fathers each year. The difference in perceived comfort with each parent is quite substantial, with close to 60% reporting comfort with the mother and only about a third indicating such a positive relationship with the father. With age, adolescents are considered better able to understand their parents' point of view, and relations at home sometimes become less conflictual (Steinberg, 1990; Youniss & Smollar, 1985). However, Table 3.1 shows that the proportion of young people who report comfortable relationships with their mothers and fathers in the aggregate remains quite stable over the 3-year period.

Comfortable relationships with friends are highly prevalent—as many adolescents find comfort with friends as with mothers. Finding comfort with friends is reported more frequently over time. Because peer friendship increases in importance during adolescence and adolescents may acquire stronger interpersonal skills as they mature, this apparent change is not surprising. The majority of adolescents likewise feel comfortable in the school setting, as indicated by perceived support from teachers and low levels of stress in meeting coursework deadlines.

The small decline in the percentage of students who consider time pressures to be low (i.e., school demands on time are manageable and therefore comfortable) could be an indication that coursework becomes more demanding for some students between the freshman and junior years of high school. However, greater involvement in activities outside the school may foster the increasing perception that there is not enough time available to complete assignments.

Many adolescents hold paid jobs during the school year: 52% of 9th graders, 47% of 10th graders, and 58% of 11th graders were employed at each annual survey. Describing comfort at work and trends in comfort over time is more challenging than in the other spheres given the variety of measures and their distributions, as well as changing sample composition. Of the employed adolescents who had supervisors, a minority (more than one third each year) report comfort with them, as indicated by feeling close to their supervisors and perceiving a willingness on the part of the supervisor to listen to problems and help find solutions. Also, a minority—approximately 40% of the working adolescents—feel extremely close or quite close to their best friend at work.

Strikingly high proportions of employed adolescents report satisfaction with work and low levels of stress. That is, approximately 85% of those who were working at the time of the annual survey indicate a high level of job satisfaction and little work stress. About 70% perceive their jobs as interesting. Taken together, employed adolescents in the Youth Development Study find their work experiences to be satisfying, nonstressful, and engaging.

In view of the widespread criticism of adolescent work, this evidence of comfort in the employment setting may seem anomalous. It should be noted, however, that for the vast majority of adolescents, the work role is more voluntary than for adults. Although some youth must work to help their families or to maintain themselves in the absence or deficiency of parental financial support, adolescents who do not want to be employed generally do not have to be. Moreover, because for the most part their material needs are provided by parents, adolescents are freer than adults to disrupt their employment to seek new jobs to obtain more satisfying work situations.

In summary, as gauged by the measures of interpersonal support, the majority of adolescents appear to be comfortable in their relationships with their mothers, teachers, and friends. However, only a minority—about a third of the youth in this study—report feelings of comfort with fathers and with supervisors at work. With respect to the task-related measures of comfort, the majority of adolescents feel comfortable with coursework expectations at school, reporting an absence of time pressures, and those who are employed are generally comfortable in their experiences at work.

DIFFERENCES IN COMFORT ACROSS GROUPS

To investigate subgroup differences in the distribution of comfort, difference-of-proportions (two-tailed) tests, a special case of the difference-of-means test (see Blalock, 1972), were performed on all dichotomous comfort measures for subgroups based on gender, race (minority vs. White), nativity (U.S.-born vs. foreign-born), parental SES (an index that combines family income and parents' educational attainment that is split at the median), and family composition (two-parent vs. other, primarily single-parent, mother-headed families). The general picture of adolescents' comfort across domains, shown in Table 3.1, serves as an aggregate baseline for the assessment of subgroup trends.

Gender

Table 3.2 displays the proportions of girls and boys experiencing comfort in each domain. Consistent with previous studies of adolescent–parent relations (Barber & Thomas, 1986; LeCroy, 1989; Steinberg, 1987), girls are significantly more comfortable with their mothers than boys in the 9th and 11th grades ($z = 2.18, p < .05; z = 7.85, p < .001$, respectively); boys are significantly more comfortable with their fathers than girls in all grades ($z = 3.79, p < .001; z = 4.51, p < .001; z = 2.29, p < .01$, respectively). Still, for both, comfort in the relation with the mother appears to be far more prevalent than that for fathers. The majority of both boys and girls report comfort in their relationships with their mothers (from 54%–63% across year and gender categories), but only a minority are comfortable with fa-

TABLE 3.2
Differences in Feelings of Comfort by Gender (Z tests)

Arena (N = 1,000)	9th Grade		10th Grade		11th Grade	
	Girls	Boys	Girls	Boys	Girls	Boys
Family comfort						
Comfort with mother	61.2	54.1*	58.5	59.7	63.0	55.6***
n	487	434	484	434	467	414
Comfort with father	29.6	42.0***	28.0	42.6***	30.4	37.9**
n	456	400	464	401	448	396
Peer comfort						
Peer support	73.6	39.7***	73.4	46.2***	75.9	54.1***
n	485	436	455	398	502	442
School comfort						
Teacher support	56.2	59.8	53.6	59.1	55.5	60.6
n	523	470	506	443	481	411
Low time pressures	70.5	65.6	68.2	63.0	62.1	60.1
n	525	471	506	443	480	411
Work comfort						
Supervisor support	44.1	38.1	38.4	28.9	41.0	28.6**
n	143	126	185	152	278	213
Support from coworker	43.6	34.4	50.8	40.1*	45.5	31.1**
n	287	160	185	152	264	212
Work satisfaction	85.4	83.4	85.5	85.3	87.4	88.6
n	322	181	262	184	317	237
Low work stress	93.0	83.4**	89.1	83.1	86.6	80.3
n	316	175	257	183	313	234
Work is interesting	75.6	70.6	70.9	71.0	69.7	68.8
n	324	180	265	186	317	237

Note. Girls (*n* = 528), employed girls (*n* ranges 266–331).
Boys (*n* = 482), employed boys (*n* ranges 186–237).
*p < .05. **p < .01. ***p < .001.

thers (28%–43%). The figures indicate a greater difference in the quality of girls' relationships with mothers and fathers than is the case for boys.

Consistent with a prior study of adolescent friendships (Savin-Williams & Berndt, 1990), higher proportions of girls than boys report close and comfortable peer friendships throughout high school; this difference is significant in the 9th, 10th, and 11th grades ($z = 10.99, p < .001; z = 8.37, p < .001; z = 7.16, p < .001$, respectively). Approximately three fourths of girls say they have a friend they can turn to, and there is little change across years. The percentage of boys who feel they have a supportive friend steadily increases over the 3-year period (from 40%–54%); however, boys are far less likely than girls to perceive such support even in the 11th grade. Girls and boys report the same propensity to find comfort in the school arena.

More girls than boys are employed, especially in the ninth grade, when 63% of girls but only 40% of boys have jobs (corresponding figures are 52 vs. 42 and 63 vs. 53 in the 10th and 11th grades). There are no significant gender differences in the proportion of employed adolescents who are comfortable with their supervisors. However, mirroring girls' greater comfort with friends generally, girls report more positive relations with friends at work in the 10th and 11th grades ($z = 1.97, p < .05; z = 3.25, p < .01$, respectively). Providing some further evidence that work may be a more positive arena for girls than for boys, girls perceive less stress in the workplace in the ninth grade ($z = 3.04, p < .01$). Girls and boys find their work to be similarly satisfying and interesting.

Parental Socioeconomic Status

Table 3.3 addresses differences in comfort based on SES. Do adolescents from more advantaged families experience higher levels of comfort in the family, peer group, school, and at work? Adolescents whose family SES is at or above the median for the sample are defined as *advantaged*, compared with adolescents whose family income is below the sample median. Some may argue that this is not a stringent enough marker of disadvantage, perhaps giving preference to criteria such as the federal poverty level. Others such as Garbarino (1992) argued that subjective perceptions of disadvantage have a greater impact on self-concept and adjustment than objective measures of poverty. Many adolescents may be unaware of their family's actual income, but are likely aware of their family's relative standing in the social status hierarchy. Therefore, we opted for a measure of disadvantage that combines household income and parental education.

Information regarding socioeconomic background was collected directly from parents in 1988, the first year of the study. An index was created that combines a standardized measure of household income with a standardized measure of parental education attainment. Parents reported their educational attainment ranging from *less than high school education* (1) to *Ph.D. or professional degree* (8). When educational attainment data are available for both mothers and fathers, their average attainment is calculated and standardized to combine with household income. Youth falling into the upper or lower half of the panel's socioeconomic structure, as gauged by this index, were compared.

Comfort with mothers and fathers does not appear to differ much by socioeconomic background; only in the 11th grade, adolescents of higher status are more comfortable with their fathers than adolescents from less advantaged homes ($z = 2.28, p < .05$). There are no significant differences in perceptions of comfort with teachers or friends. School pressures are also experienced to the same extent for both groups. Although there is some indication that students of lower SES feel less time pressure, this dif-

TABLE 3.3
Differences in Feelings of Comfort by Parental
Socioeconomic Status: Split at Median (Z tests)

Arena (N = 1,000)	9th Grade		10th Grade		11th Grade	
	Low	High	Low	High	Low	High
Family comfort						
Comfort with mother	58.0	57.7	57.7	60.4	57.0	61.9
n	469	452	456	462	435	446
Comfort with father	34.7	36.0	31.9	37.5	30.0	37.4*
n	412	444	414	451	403	441
Peer comfort						
Peer support	54.9	60.3	60.5	61.0	64.5	66.9
n	468	453	420	433	476	468
School comfort						
Teacher support	57.9	57.9	55.1	57.3	56.0	59.6
n	515	478	481	468	434	458
Low time pressures	70.8	65.3	67.8	63.7	65.6	57.0**
n	518	478	481	468	433	458
Work comfort						
Supervisor support	40.8	41.8	33.1	35.2	31.1	40.0
n	147	122	178	159	241	250
Support from coworker	42.7	37.9	47.5	44.3	37.6	40.5
n	220	227	179	158	234	242
Work satisfaction	85.0	84.4	85.7	85.1	85.3	90.4
n	246	257	224	222	272	282
Low work stress	87.2	92.0	83.3	89.9*	82.5	85.3
n	242	249	222	218	268	279
Work is interesting	72.9	74.7	66.7	75.3*	69.6	69.0
n	247	257	228	223	273	281

Note. Low socioeconomic status youth (*n* = 530), employed low socioeconomic status youth (*n* ranges 229–273).

High socioeconomic status youth (*n* = 480), employed high socioeconomic status youth (*n* ranges 225–283)

*$p < .05$. **$p < .01$. ***$p < .001$.

ference is only statistically significant in the 11th grade ($z = 2.64, p < .01$). Doing well in school could become particularly important during the latter part of high school for students of higher socioeconomic level who plan, or are expected, to go to college.

In the work arena, two significant differences emerge: In the 10th grade, a greater proportion of adolescents from more advantaged homes report that work stress is low ($z = 2.04, p < .05$) and that work is interesting ($z = 2.02, p < .05$). Although differences are not consistent across years, adolescents from higher socioeconomic homes appear to have somewhat more comfortable work experiences than adolescents from less advantaged families.

Minority Status

In their study of Black and White adolescents' self-esteem, Simmons and colleagues (Simmons, Brown, Bush, & Blyth, 1978) found that relationships with parents and friends are supportive and promote positive self-images in both groups. It is reasonable to suppose that school and work would be less comfortable for minority adolescents, in comparison to their White counterparts, due to racial discrimination and perceptions of constrained opportunities. However, for the most part, minority and White adolescents in our study do not differ in their reports of comfort in any of the four arenas (data not shown).

Because sample size is limited (only 74 adolescents in the initial panel were born outside the United States), caution is advised in reviewing Table 3.4, which reports comfort differences by nativity. Subgroup compari-

TABLE 3.4
Differences in Feelings of Comfort by Nativity:
Foreign- Versus U.S.-Born (Z tests)

	9th Grade		10th Grade		11th Grade	
Arena (N = 1,000)	Foreign	U.S.	Foreign	U.S.	Foreign	U.S.
Family comfort						
Comfort with mother	55.9	58.0	55.4	59.0	59.3	59.7
n	68	833	65	834	59	804
Comfort with father	43.9	34.9	44.3	33.8	40.4	33.7
n	57	784	61	787	57	768
Peer comfort						
Peer support	49.2	58.1	59.3	61.0	52.4	66.7*
n	65	844	59	776	63	859
School comfort						
Teacher support	58.1	57.9	67.1	55.0	64.1	57.5
n	74	900	70	858	64	809
Low time pressures	63.5	68.6	60.9	66.2	55.6	61.6
n	74	902	69	860	63	809
Work comfort						
Supervisor support	18.8	42.3*	39.1	33.7	41.4	35.4
n	16	246	23	306	29	455
Support from coworker	45.0	39.6	42.1	45.6	18.5	40.4**
n	20	417	19	309	27	441
Work satisfaction	78.3	84.6	84.0	85.5	82.4	88.2
n	23	469	25	408	34	510
Low work stress	82.6	89.9	80.0	86.6	81.8	83.7
n	23	457	25	402	33	504
Work is interesting	79.2	73.3	65.4	70.9	67.6	69.4
n	24	469	26	412	34	510

Note. Foreign-born youth (n = 74), employed foreign-born youth (n ranges 24–34). U.S.-born youth (n = 906), employed U.S.-born youth (n ranges 415–512).
*p < .05. **p < .01. ***p < .001.

sons involving the work arena are particularly questionable because so few immigrant adolescents were employed (24–34) in any given year. Still the unique adaptive pressures placed on foreign-born adolescents make it instructive to compare their perceptions of comfort with their native-born counterparts.

As shown in the first two rows of Table 3.4, immigrant adolescents are no more comfortable with their mothers and fathers than native-born adolescents. They appear to be less comfortable with friends during high school, but this difference only reaches significance in the 11th grade ($z = 2.19, p < .05$). Immigrant students are not significantly more likely to report feeling comfortable at school than native-born students.

Within the work arena, more U.S.-born adolescents report being comfortable with their supervisor than foreign-born workers in the ninth grade ($z = 2.22, p < .05$). However, perceptions of support from supervisors are essentially the same for foreign- and U.S.-born adolescents in the following 2 years of high school. In the 11th grade, American-born workers are significantly more comfortable with their friends at work than foreign-born employees (40.4% compared with 18.5% for immigrants, $z = 2.75, p < .01$). Otherwise, foreign- and U.S.-born adolescents appear to perceive similar levels of work stress and seem equally satisfied with, and interested in, their work.

Family Structure

Although significant differences are not found in all years, comfort with mothers and fathers appears to be higher for adolescents living in two-parent homes (including both intact and blended families) than for adolescents living in other situations (comprised of 66.3% mother-headed, single-parent families, 7.7% father-headed, single-parent families, 8% joint custody arrangements, and 17.9% living with other relatives, in foster homes, or another arrangement). As shown in Table 3.5, 10th- and 11th-grade adolescents in two-parent families are significantly more comfortable with their mothers than adolescents in other living arrangements ($z = 2.48$ and $z = 2.37$, respectively; $p < .05$). Similarly, 11th graders in two-parent families are more comfortable with their fathers ($z = 2.80, p < .01$). The percentage of adolescents described as comfortable with friends and in school does not vary by family composition.

For the most part, relationships and experiences at work are similar for adolescents in two-parent families and other family forms. Employed adolescents have similarly comfortable relationships with their supervisor and best friend at work regardless of family composition. In addition, similar proportions of adolescents in both groups regard their work as satisfying. However, where a difference in comfort in the work setting is apparent, it

TABLE 3.5
Differences in Feelings of Comfort by Family Composition (Z tests)

Arena (N = 1,000)	9th Grade		10th Grade		11th Grade	
	Two-Parent	Other	Two-Parent	Other	Two-Parent	Other
Family comfort						
Comfort with mother	57.5	58.9	61.6	52.7*	62.1	53.5*
n	668	253	643	273	609	269
Comfort with father	36.5	31.6	35.7	32.0	36.6	26.8*
n	666	190	644	219	606	235
Peer comfort						
Peer support	57.7	57.1	60.4	61.5	66.3	64.4
n	631	287	584	265	605	334
School comfort						
Teacher support	59.3	55.3	57.3	53.6	56.6	60.0
n	678	311	640	304	583	305
Low time pressures	68.8	67.1	65.1	67.2	59.7	63.8
n	679	313	639	305	583	304
Work comfort						
Supervisor support	41.6	41.5	35.1	32.4	34.4	37.6
n	185	82	231	105	331	157
Support from coworker	41.0	39.2	44.1	51.0	36.3	44.7
n	315	130	236	100	322	152
Work satisfaction	83.7	87.5	86.0	84.0	87.9	87.8
n	356	144	314	131	371	181
Low work stress	91.6	84.4	87.8	84.4	86.1	79.9
n	347	141	311	128	366	179
Work is interesting	72.4	78.2	73.6	64.4	71.9	63.5*
n	359	142	318	132	370	181

Note. Youth in two-parent homes (*n* ranges 613–681), employed youth in two-parent homes (*n* ranges 319–371).

Youth living in other family situations (*n* ranges 312–339), employed youth living in other family situations (*n* ranges 134–182).

*$p < .05$. **$p < .01$. ***$p < .001$.

is in favor of youth from two-parent families. Specifically, in the 11th grade, workers from two-parent families are somewhat more likely to feel their work is interesting ($z = 1.96, p < .05$).

THE NUMBER OF ARENAS PERCEIVED AS COMFORTABLE

We now examine the number of arenas, among those available to the adolescent, that are perceived as comfortable, as well as differences in the subgroups under consideration in the prevalence of comfort across settings.

As described in chapter 2, one indicator of comfort (an interpersonal, support-oriented comfort measure) from each arena was used to represent comfort in an additive comfort index. Comfort in the family setting is assessed by whether the adolescent has a positive, supportive relationship with at least one parent. Measures of comfort at school and with friends are single items indicating perceptions of the accessibility of support from a teacher and friends, respectively. The measure of work comfort is whether the employed adolescent has a warm relationship with a best friend at work and/or with a supervisor.

In an attempt to summarize the scope of comfort in a manner that would be applicable to both workers and nonworkers, we examine the proportion of arenas rated as comfortable among those available to the adolescent. That is, given the scope of our study, employed adolescents may find comfort in as many as four arenas (i.e., family, school, peer, and work), whereas nonworking adolescents may be comfortable in only up to three contexts. Score values range from 0, designating no arenas of comfort, to 6, indicating comfort in all four arenas for workers and comfort for nonworkers in the three arenas available to them.

The percent distribution of comfort index scores is shown for the total panel each year in Table 3.6. A minority of adolescents (over the 3-year period, between 9%–11%) do not report comfort in any arena—they lack comfort with a parent, friend, teacher, work supervisor, or work friend. As discussed earlier, because we do not assess all possible comfort arenas in

TABLE 3.6
Comfort Index for the Total Panel

Variable	9th Grade	10th Grade	11th Grade
0 (W & NW, zero comfort arenas)	8.3	9.4	7.2
1 (W, comfort in 1/4 arenas)	10.1	9.4	10.9
2 (NW, comfort in 1/3 arenas)	14.5	15.4	11.5
3 (W, comfort in 2/4 arenas)	16.1	14.3	17.6
4 (NW, comfort in 2/3 arenas)	20.0	19.5	15.9
5 (W, comfort in 3/4 arenas)	15.8 → 66.0	13.9 → 65.8	16.9 → 70.4
6 (W & NW, comfort in all arenas)	15.1	18.1	20.0
N	991	958	955
Mean	3.4	3.4	3.5
Mode	4.0	4.0	6.0
Median	4.0	4.0	4.0
Standard deviation	1.8	1.9	1.9

Note. W = workers (employed adolescents), NW = nonworkers.

the Youth Development Study, these adolescents are not necessarily bereft of support. Nonetheless, they are missing such support in what are clearly quite important spheres in adolescents' lives.

Most adolescents find comfort, as we have defined it, in at least one arena. A large proportion of adolescents are comfortable in at least half of the arenas available to them. As highlighted in Table 3.6, in any given year, more than 65% of the adolescents feel supported by others in two or more contexts. Insofar as a trend can be discerned, the number of arenas perceived as comfortable appears to increase slightly over time. For example, a growing proportion of adolescents find comfort in all of the arenas assessed (increasing from 15% in the 9th grade to 20% in the 11th grade).

As shown in Table 3.7, in each of the 3 years, girls are found to be comfortable in a greater number of arenas than boys (as indicated by a difference in means test, reported consecutively: $t = 5.09, p < .001; t = 2.80, p < .01; t = 4.52, p < .001$). As highlighted in the table, a larger proportion of girls than boys are clustered at the upper end of the distribution each year. For example, in the ninth grade, 74% of girls, but only 59% of boys, find comfort in two or more of the arenas available to them. Furthermore, each year a smaller proportion of girls than boys do not find support in any of the measured arenas; a larger percentage of girls than boys are comfortable in 100% of the contexts to which they have access.

Although boys tend to experience comfort in fewer domains than girls, for boys the number of arenas defined as comfortable increases somewhat over time. As shown in the lower panel, 59.2% of 9th-grade boys perceive comfort in two or more arenas; 65.2% do so in the 11th grade. However, the percentage of boys reporting no support declines negligibly over time.

Adolescents from higher socioeconomic backgrounds appear to be comfortable in a greater number of arenas than less advantaged adolescents (see Table 3.8). Especially in Grades 10 and 11, more adolescents from economically advantaged homes are comfortable in 100% of the arenas assessed. As shown in the table, a somewhat larger percentage of adolescents from higher socioeconomic families are distributed at the upper end of the index (i.e., comfortable in two or more arenas). However, tests of significance indicate this difference is only statistically significant in the 11th grade ($t = 2.99, p < .01$).

Adolescents living in two-parent families are comfortable in a larger number of arenas than their counterparts in other living situations (see Table 3.9); this difference reaches significance in Grades 10 and 11 (reported consecutively: $t = 2.16, p < .05; t = 2.09, p < .05$; see Table 3.9). Moreover, each year more of the adolescents in two-parent families are clustered at the higher end of the comfort arenas index. For example, in

TABLE 3.7
Comfort Index for Girls and Boys

Girls	9th Grade	10th Grade	11th Grade
0 (W & NW, zero comfort arenas)	5.0	7.3	5.7
1 (W, comfort in 1/4 arenas)	11.7	10.6	8.9
2 (NW, comfort in 1/3 arenas)	9.2	13.5	10.5
3 (W, comfort in 2/4 arenas)	18.4	15.5	17.8
4 (NW, comfort in 2/3 arenas)	17.4	15.9	13.0
5 (W, comfort in 3/4 arenas)	20.1 → 74.3	16.1 → 68.7	19.9 → 75.0
6 (W & NW, comfort in all arenas)	18.4	21.2	24.3
N	523	510	507
Mean	3.7	3.6	3.8
Mode	5.0	6.0	6.0
Median	4.0	4.0	4.0
Standard deviation	1.8	1.9	1.9

Boys	9th Grade	10th Grade	11th Grade
0 (W & NW, zero comfort arenas)	12.0	11.8	8.9
1 (W, comfort in 1/4 arenas)	8.3	8.0	13.2
2 (NW, comfort in 1/3 arenas)	20.5	17.6	12.7
3 (W, comfort in 2/4 arenas)	13.7	12.9	17.4
4 (NW, comfort in 2/3 arenas)	22.9	23.7	19.2
5 (W, comfort in 3/4 arenas)	11.1 → 59.2	11.4 → 62.5	13.4 → 65.2
6 (W & NW, comfort in all arenas)	11.5	14.5	15.2
N	468	448	448
Mean	3.1	3.2	3.3
Mode	4.0	4.0	4.0
Median	3.0	3.0	3.0
Standard deviation	1.8	1.9	1.9

Note. W = workers (employed adolescents), NW = nonworkers.

the ninth grade, just over 68% of adolescents in two-parent homes are comfortable in two or more arenas, compared with 64.8% of adolescents living in other family forms. Furthermore, the modal category on the comfort index is higher each year for adolescents in two-parent families. For example, in the 10th grade, the largest concentration of adolescents in two-parent homes is in Category 6, indicating comfort in all available arenas; it is Category 4, indicating comfort in only two of three arenas, for adolescents living in other situations.

TABLE 3.8
Comfort Index for Higher and Lower Socioeconomic
Homes (Split at the Median)

High Socioeconomic Status	9th Grade		10th Grade		11th Grade	
0 (W & NW, zero comfort arenas)	7.1		9.1		6.6	
1 (W, comfort in 1/4 arenas)	10.1		8.3		11.4	
2 (NW, comfort in 1/3 arenas)	13.7		15.7		9.1	
3 (W, comfort in 2/4 arenas)	17.9		15.3		15.2	
4 (NW, comfort in 2/3 arenas)	18.7		17.8		15.2	
5 (W, comfort in 3/4 arenas)	16.8	→ 69.2	13.2	→ 66.9	18.2	→ 72.9
6 (W & NW, comfort in all arenas)	15.8		20.6		24.3	
N	476		471		473	
Mean	3.4		3.5		3.7	
Mode	4.0		6.0		6.0	
Median	4.0		4.0		4.0	
Standard deviation	1.8		1.9		1.9	

Low Socioeconomic Status	9th Grade		10th Grade		11th Grade	
0 (W & NW, zero comfort arenas)	9.3		9.7		7.9	
1 (W, comfort in 1/4 arenas)	10.1		10.5		10.4	
2 (NW, comfort in 1/3 arenas)	15.3		15.2		13.9	
3 (W, comfort in 2/4 arenas)	14.6		13.3		19.9	
4 (NW, comfort in 2/3 arenas)	21.2		21.1		16.6	
5 (W, comfort in 3/4 arenas)	15.0	→ 65.4	14.6	→ 64.6	15.6	→ 67.9
6 (W & NW, comfort in all arenas)	14.6		15.6		15.8	
N	515		487		482	
Mean	3.3		3.3		3.4	
Mode	4.0		4.0		3.0	
Median	4.0		4.0		3.0	
Standard deviation	1.8		1.9		1.8	

Note. W = workers (employed adolescents), NW = nonworkers.

Minority and foreign-born adolescents find comfort across a similar proportion of arenas as the White and native-born adolescents (data not shown).

Thus, as predicted, girls perceive comfort across a greater number of arenas than boys, although over time the gender difference is diminished by boys' increasing comfort across a variety of settings. In addition, there is some evidence that more advantaged adolescents—those from higher

TABLE 3.9
Comfort Index for Two-Parent and Other Families
(Primarily Single-Parent Families)

Two-Parent Families	9th Grade	10th Grade	11th Grade
0 (W & NW, zero comfort arenas)	7.8	9.0	6.4
1 (W, comfort in 1/4 arenas)	10.0	8.4	12.1
2 (NW, comfort in 1/3 arenas)	13.6	14.2	10.0
3 (W, comfort in 2/4 arenas)	17.0	15.7	16.0
4 (NW, comfort in 2/3 arenas)	19.2	18.4	15.8
5 (W, comfort in 3/4 arenas)	15.5 → 68.5	14.8 → 68.5	18.1 → 71.6
6 (W & NW, comfort in all arenas)	16.8	19.6	21.7
N	677	643	613
Mean	3.4	3.5	3.6
Mode	4.0	6.0	6.0
Median	4.0	4.0	4.0
Standard deviation	1.8	1.9	1.9

Other Family Forms	9th Grade	10th Grade	11th Grade
0 (W & NW, zero comfort arenas)	9.0	10.0	8.9
1 (W, comfort in 1/4 arenas)	9.4	11.6	8.9
2 (NW, comfort in 1/3 arenas)	16.8	18.1	14.5
3 (W, comfort in 2/4 arenas)	14.5	11.3	10.1
4 (NW, comfort in 2/3 arenas)	21.9	21.6	16.0
5 (W, comfort in 3/4 arenas)	16.8 → 64.8	12.3 → 60.4	14.8 → 67.8
6 (W & NW, comfort in all arenas)	11.6	15.2	16.9
N	310	310	338
Mean	3.3	3.2	3.4
Mode	4.0	4.0	3.0
Median	4.0	3.0	3.0
Standard deviation	1.8	1.9	1.9

Note. W = workers (employed adolescents), NW = nonworkers.

socioeconomic homes and those who live with two parents—perceive more sources of comfort and support.

SUMMARY AND CONCLUSIONS

This chapter presents a rather salutary picture: Adolescents in the Youth Development Study find comfort in a variety of settings. In fact, comfort appears to be much more prevalent than discomfort; very few perceive little support by adults or peers in family, school, friendship, or workplace settings. Mothers are a source of comfort for the majority of adolescents; consistent with prior research (Steinberg, 1990), more adolescents report positive, supportive relationships with their mothers than with their fathers (LeCroy, 1989; Steinberg, 1987). The majority of adolescents also find comfort in relationships with friends (Csikszentmihalyi & Larson, 1984; Savin-Williams & Berndt, 1990). Although there are surely obstacles to establishing close relationships with adults at school (Csikszentmihalyi & Larson, 1984; Eccles et al., 1997; Simmons & Blyth, 1987), most adolescents likewise report comfortable, supportive relations with their teachers. In addition, they feel comfortable with their coursework obligations.

When they are employed, adolescents find satisfaction in their work and find it rewarding and relatively free of stress. However, experiencing comfort in relationships with work supervisors and friends is less prevalent. Given the high degree of turnover in adolescents' jobs, establishing close relationships at work may be difficult.

The findings support prior research on gender differences. For example, girls are more comfortable with their mothers and boys are more comfortable with their fathers. Girls also perceive their relationships with their friends to be closer and more comfortable than boys (see Csikszentmihalyi & Larson, 1984; Savin-Williams & Berndt, 1990). Although there is some indication that girls perceive work to be more stressful than boys, girls are more comfortable with their best friends at work (see Mortimer et al., 1992a, 1992b).

Generally, despite reasons to expect that the more advantaged adolescents would be more likely to experience comfort, there were relatively few significant differences when each domain was examined singly by family socioeconomic background, race, nativity, or family structure. For example, SES was not associated with disparities in comfort with mothers, friends, teachers, or friends at work in any year. The few significant differences were generally in the expected direction, but these were not manifest across years. For example, only 11th-grade adolescents from higher socioeconomic households reported more comfort in their relations with their fathers. Only two significant differences by socioeconomic level emerged in the work arena (of 15 comparisons). Similarly, minority adolescents were as comfortable as White adolescents at home, with friends, at school, and at work. There were only a few scattered differences between native- and foreign-born adolescents.

Examination of the number of contexts in which adolescents feel comfortable yielded a similarly positive assessment of the prevalence of comfort in adolescents' lives. Most adolescents are comfortable in at least one context (approximately 90%); the majority (more than 60%) find comfort in two or more arenas. Adolescent girls are comfortable in a larger num-

ber of arenas than boys, lending further testimony to adolescent girls'
greater interpersonal or communal orientation. However, it appears that
the number of arenas described as comfortable increases somewhat for
boys over time.

Insofar as we find support for the expectation that objective advantage
will be reflected in subjective comfort, it arises from assessment of the
summary "comfort index." That is, adolescents from higher socioeconomic backgrounds and those who live in two-parent families perceive
comfort in more arenas than adolescents from less advantaged and less
conventional families, respectively. These subgroup differences provide
some indication that perceptions of comfort are shaped by larger societal
forces. As Simmons (in press) suggested, people differ in their propensity
to view the world as comfortable, and this propensity is shaped, at least in
part, by their position in the social structure.

Almost all adolescents in the panel indicate social support and/or satisfying experiences in at least one domain; most have two or more sources
of comfort. However, there are clear differences in the panel as a whole,
and between particular subgroups, in the number of arenas experienced
as comfortable. The next chapter examines the consequences of such
differences for adolescents' psychological adjustment and academic performance.

CHAPTER FOUR

Arenas of Comfort
and Adolescent Adjustment

People have multiple identities, participate in diverse role-relationships, and circulate among several different contexts daily. Identifying arenas of comfort, as well as those contexts that mainly yield feelings of discomfort, presumes a degree of complexity in individual lives. Simmons and Blyth (1987) contended that, in most cases, the more contexts and role-relationships the adolescent is invested in, the more favorable are the consequences for mental health and adjustment. According to their reasoning, the person's sense of personal worth and importance increases with the number of arenas of participation, especially when the person finds supportive others in those contexts. Simmons (in press) qualified this by noting that it is better to have distinct role-partners in different setting, and she acknowledged the potential for role strain.

Thoits (1983) found that adults who report more social identities scored higher on indicators of psychological adjustment than adults with fewer. Following the work of Merton (1968) and Stryker (1980), Thoits (1983) explained that social identities are created and maintained in reciprocal role-relationships that "give purpose, meaning, direction, and guidance to one's life. The greater the number of identities held, the stronger one's sense of meaningful, guided existence" (p. 175). Supportive and accepting role-partners are especially consequential for psychological health (Cauce et al., 1982; Compas, Slavin, et al., 1986; Robinson & Garber, 1995; Simmons & Blyth, 1987; Windle, 1992).

Multiple contexts of action may also yield mental health benefits because of their capacity to buffer negative interactions or activities in other domains. Having multiple contexts of action increases the likelihood that stressors or disruption in one arena can be buffered by involvement and support in another (Lepore, 1992; Linville, 1985; Thoits, 1983). As arenas of involvement are more numerous, it becomes more likely that at least one will be satisfying. As a result, when there are more role-relationships (and domain-relevant activities) available to the person, the more readily change or discomfort in any one role can be tolerated. We address this hypothesis directly in chapter 5.

The first question addressed in this chapter is whether cumulative experiences of comfort matter for adolescent mental health and achievement. Does such comfort have positive consequences for the self-concept, as indicated by higher self-esteem and mastery, and lower levels of self-derogation? Does it influence the adolescent's mood state, feelings of well-being, and depressive affect? How does it affect the adolescent's performance in school?

Although Simmons (in press; Simmons & Blyth, 1987) emphasized the problems inherent in the total absence of comfort, only a minority of adolescents reported that they lacked comfort in all four observed domains of family, peers, school, and work. (As shown in the previous chapter, less than 10% lacked an arena of comfort in any of the 3 years of observation.) We therefore investigate whether advantages accrue to adolescents who have more arenas of comfort in comparison to those with fewer. Does social support have a cumulative effect when experienced in multiple domains? Some sources of comfort may have relevance for particular developmental needs. For example, the peer group is thought to provide opportunities for growth in interpersonal skills and self-knowledge that are not available in the family setting (Csikszentmihalyi & Larson, 1984; Douvan & Adelson, 1966; Erikson, 1968; Rosenberg, 1979). If this is the case, then youth with more diverse comfort arenas would likely have a broader range of needs that are fulfilled and, hence, better mental health and achievement.

Furthermore, we assess gender differences. Do boys and girls experience the same benefits from a larger number of supportive relations? If girls are indeed more sensitive to the quality of their interpersonal relationships than boys (Douvan & Adelson, 1966; Gilligan, 1982; Richards & Larson, 1989), they may be more responsive to both positive and negative social interactions. In fact, there is evidence that adult women benefit more than men from social support (Wethington & Kessler, 1986). Conversely, women experience greater psychological distress as a result of negative social relationships (Schuster et al., 1990).

It is also fruitful to examine whether comfort in any particular context is more consequential to adolescents' mental health and achievement than that experienced in others, and whether the various sources of comfort differ in their impacts over time. Although adolescents with access to multiple social supports may have greater psychological health and higher levels of achievement than those with fewer, it is possible that some sources of support are more salutary than others (Lepore, 1992). Some influences may also be specific to particular contexts and outcomes. For example, it is reasonable to presume that supportive relations with teachers would be especially important in sustaining high academic achievement.

Therefore, after assessing the effects of cumulative comfort across domains of involvement, this chapter addresses the relative impacts of perceived support from parents, friends, teachers, supervisors, and/or work peers. Based on the substantial empirical evidence testifying to the importance of parental relationships to adolescents' adjustment (Emery & Kitzmann, 1995; Gecas & Seff, 1991; Jessor & Jessor, 1977; LeCroy, 1989; Maccoby et al., 1983; Mortimer et al., 1986; Steinberg & Silverberg, 1986), supportive relationships in the family arena are expected to have pervasive consequences.

Peer relations should also be of great consequence to psychological adjustment given the increased salience of friendship and the growing amounts of time spent with friends at this time of life (Csikszentmihalyi & Larson, 1984). The highly discretionary character of adolescent friendships (Hartup, 1983) would perhaps heighten peers' psychological salience. Particularly when relationships with parents are strained, adolescents turn to friends for support and guidance (Galambos & Ehrenberg, 1997; Savin-Williams & Berndt, 1990). In light of the more transient nature of affiliations and experiences in school and work, it is anticipated that comfort in these settings will be less predictive of adolescent mental health.

CUMULATIVE ARENAS OF COMFORT
AND ADOLESCENT ADJUSTMENT

In an initial assessment of whether arenas of comfort have positive developmental consequences, we inspect the zero-order relationships between the proportion of comfortable arenas and the mental health and achievement outcomes during 3 years of high school (Grades 9–11). Specifically, we examine differences, by scores on the comfort index, in mean levels of well-being, self-derogation, self-esteem, depressive affect, mastery, and grade point average (GPA; using one-way analysis of variance [ANOVA]). Scheffe multiple-group comparison tests were also performed to identify significant differences between categories.

In the total panel, most associations between the comfort index scores and the adjustment indicators were found to be statistically significant (with the exceptions of depressive affect in the 9th grade and GPA in the

10th grade). That is, adolescents' mental health and academic perform-ance were positively associated with the proportion of arenas deemed comfortable. Inspection of the means revealed generally monotonic changes for each unit increase on the comfort arenas index, with little sug-gestion of curvilinear effects.

For example, Table 4.1 shows the differences in self-esteem each year in the total panel by the score on the comfort index. Mean levels of self-esteem are significantly associated with the index on each occasion ($p < .001$), and there are significant differences between particular subcate-gories as well. There is a clear tendency, each year, for self-esteem to in-crease with the proportion of arenas deemed comfortable. Notably, how-ever, adolescents with only one arena of comfort do not have significantly higher self-esteem than those who report no comfort arenas. Significant benefit is only apparent once comfort is obtained in two or more arenas. Moreover, at the upper end of the distribution, having comfort in all areas does not seem to confer additional benefit beyond feeling comfortable in most areas (2 of 3, or 3 of 4). A similar pattern is manifest for well-being and mastery (Tables 4.2 and 4.3). Self-derogation, depressive affect, and GPA are less clearly related in the sample as a whole to the comfort index (Tables 4.4, 4.5, and 4.6).

However, if gender conditions the relationship between comfort and adjustment, examining this association in the total panel could obscure key influences. Although adolescent girls' vulnerability to derogating self-perceptions (Menaghan, 1990; Simmons & Blyth, 1987) and depres-sion (Compas et al., 1998; Petersen, Sargiani, & Kennedy, 1991) is often observed, we focus here on gender differences in the effects of comfort (although as we see, the mean differences make boys' psychological ad-vantage clearly apparent). Given reasons to expect that gender would moderate the influence of social support, the key constituent of the com-fort index, we examine associations between this index and adjustment separately for boys and girls.

Analyses by gender show that differences in self-esteem are significantly related to the arenas of comfort index for both genders; the greater the proportion of comfort arenas, the higher boys' and girls' self-esteem. Fig-ure 4.1 indicates that the relationship between arenas of comfort and self-esteem is more pronounced among the girls than among the boys (the gender difference in effect is statistically significant, $p < .01$, in the 11th grade, and of borderline significance, $p = .065$, in the 10th grade). Whereas girls with multiple arenas of comfort are found to have a level of self-esteem that is comparable to that of the boys, girls with few comfort arenas have substantially lower self-esteem than comparable boys.

Both genders' sense of mastery improves when comfort is experienced across multiple arenas; there are no significant gender differences in effect

TABLE 4.1
Mean Self-Esteem by Comfort Index (Total Panel)

Comfort Arenas Index	9th Grade								10th Grade								11th Grade							
	0	1	2	3	4	5	6	Mean	0	1	2	3	4	5	6	Mean	0	1	2	3	4	5	6	Mean
0 (W & NW, zero comfort arenas)								12.60								12.20								12.23
1 (W, comfort in 1/4 arenas)								13.17								12.81								12.97
2 (NW, comfort in 1/3 arenas)								13.24								13.12								13.28
3 (W, comfort in 2/4 arenas)	*							13.29	*							13.94	*							13.47
4 (NW, comfort in 2/3 arenas)	*							13.90	*	*						14.08	*	*						14.05
5 (W, comfort in 3/4 arenas)	*							14.03	*	*						14.07	*	*	*					14.51
6 (W & NW, comfort in all arenas)	*	*	*	*				14.35	*	*	*					14.47	*	*	*	*				14.60
Grand mean								13.62								13.69								13.80
F (Number of cases)	$F = 8.03, p < .001$							(965)	$F = 12.88, p < .001$							(945)	$F = 13.86, p < .001$							(950)

Note. *denotes significant differences at $p < .05$ using Scheffe multigroup comparison test, ANOVA procedure. W = workers (employed adolescents), NW = nonworkers.

TABLE 4.2
Mean Well-Being by Comfort Index (Total Panel)

Comfort Arenas Index	9th Grade								10th Grade								11th Grade							
	0	1	2	3	4	5	6	Mean	0	1	2	3	4	5	6	Mean	0	1	2	3	4	5	6	Mean
0 (W & NW, zero comfort arenas)								14.57								14.40								13.95
1 (W, comfort in 1/4 arenas)								14.67								14.77								15.02
2 (NW, comfort in 1/3 arenas)								15.19								14.87								14.74
3 (W, comfort in 2/4 arenas)								15.63	*							15.95	*							15.56
4 (NW, comfort in 2/3 arenas)	*	*						16.24	*		*					16.10	*	*						16.18
5 (W, comfort in 3/4 arenas)	*	*	*					16.86	*	*	*					16.87	*	*	*					16.64
6 (W & NW, comfort in all arenas)	*	*	*	*				17.14	*	*	*					16.98	*	*	*	*				17.00
Grand mean								15.94								15.87								15.86
F (Number of cases)	F = 15.55, p < .001							(970)	F = 14.75, p < .001							(940)	F = 17.46, p < .001							(947)

Note. *denotes significant differences at $p < .05$ using Scheffe multigroup comparison test, ANOVA procedure.
W = workers (employed adolescents), NW = nonworkers.

TABLE 4.3
Mean Mastery by Comfort Index (Total Panel)

Comfort Arenas Index	9th Grade							Mean	10th Grade							Mean	11th Grade							Mean
	0	1	2	3	4	5	6		0	1	2	3	4	5	6		0	1	2	3	4	5	6	
0 (W & NW, zero comfort arenas)								13.27								12.73								13.25
1 (W, comfort in 1/4 arenas)								13.35								12.68								13.22
2 (NW, comfort in 1/3 arenas)								13.54								13.51								13.84
3 (W, comfort in 2/4 arenas)								13.47	*	*						14.23								14.06
4 (NW, comfort in 2/3 arenas)								14.08	*	*	*	*				14.54					*			14.54
5 (W, comfort in 3/4 arenas)								14.18	*	*	*	*				14.59	*	*						14.85
6 (W & NW, comfort in all arenas)	*	*	*	*	*			14.65	*	*	*	*				15.20	*	*	*	*				15.17
Grand mean								13.87								14.12								14.32
F (Number of cases)	$F = 5.94, p < .001$							(958)	$F = 18.23, p < .001$							(936)	$F = 11.28, p < .001$							(943)

Note. *denotes significant differences at $p < .05$ using Scheffe multigroup comparison test, ANOVA procedure.
W = workers (employed adolescents), NW = nonworkers.

TABLE 4.4
Mean Self-Derogation by Comfort Index (Total Panel)

Comfort Arenas Index	9th Grade								10th Grade								11th Grade							
	0	1	2	3	4	5	6	Mean	0	1	2	3	4	5	6	Mean	0	1	2	3	4	5	6	Mean
0 (W & NW, zero comfort arenas)								10.06								10.31								10.75
1 (W, comfort in 1/4 arenas)								9.76								10.45								10.25
2 (NW, comfort in 1/3 arenas)								9.73								9.92								9.64
3 (W, comfort in 2/4 arenas)								9.82								9.39								9.60
4 (NW, comfort in 2/3 arenas)		*						9.22		*						9.10	*							9.15
5 (W, comfort in 3/4 arenas)								9.15								9.37	*	*						8.78
6 (W & NW, comfort in all arenas)		*	*	*				9.00		*	*	*				8.57	*	*	*	*				8.42
Grand mean								9.47								9.45								9.31
F (Number of cases)	F = 3.26, p < .001							(955)	F = 8.31, p < .001							(936)	F = 10.78, p < .001							(943)

Note. —*denotes significant differences at p < .05 using Scheffe multigroup comparison test, ANOVA procedure.
W = workers (employed adolescents), NW = nonworkers.

TABLE 4.5

Mean Depressive Affect by Comfort Index (Total Panel)

Comfort Arenas Index	9th Grade								10th Grade								11th Grade							
	0	1	2	3	4	5	6	Mean	0	1	2	3	4	5	6	Mean	0	1	2	3	4	5	6	Mean
0 (W & NW, zero comfort arenas)								19.09								20.81								21.61
1 (W, comfort in 1/4 arenas)								19.88								21.20								21.14
2 (NW, comfort in 1/3 arenas)								18.45								19.85								20.16
3 (W, comfort in 2/4 arenas)								18.78								18.93								19.79
4 (NW, comfort in 2/3 arenas)								18.21			*					18.49		*	*					18.28
5 (W, comfort in 3/4 arenas)								18.32								18.67		*	*					18.35
6 (W & NW, comfort in all arenas)								17.58		*	*					17.72		*	*	*				17.59
Grand mean								18.49								19.11								19.18
F (Number of cases)	F = 1.90							(965)	F = 5.95, p < .001							(941)	F = 8.53, p < .001							(952)

Note. *denotes significant differences at p < .05 using Scheffé multigroup comparison test, ANOVA procedure. W = workers (employed adolescents), NW = nonworkers.

69

TABLE 4.6

Mean Grade Point Average by Comfort Index (Total Panel)

Comfort Arenas Index	9th Grade		10th Grade		11th Grade	
	0 1 2 3 4 5 6	Mean	0 1 2 3 4 5 6	Mean	0 1 2 3 4 5 6	Mean
0 (W & NW, zero comfort arenas)		2.30		2.45		2.44
1 (W, comfort in 1/4 arenas)		2.48		2.37		2.50
2 (NW, comfort in 1/3 arenas)		2.31		2.50		2.44
3 (W, comfort in 2/4 arenas)		2.58		2.64		2.61
4 (NW, comfort in 2/3 arenas)		2.47		2.56		2.63
5 (W, comfort in 3/4 arenas)		2.61		2.59		2.64
6 (W & NW, comfort in all arenas)		2.57		2.66		2.80
Grand mean		2.49		2.56		2.62
F (Number of cases)	$F = 2.93, p < .001$	(955)	$F = 1.850$	(930)	$F = 3.34, p < .001$	(885)

Note. *denotes significant differences at $p < .05$ using Scheffe multigroup comparison test, ANOVA procedure.
W = workers (employed adolescents), NW = nonworkers.

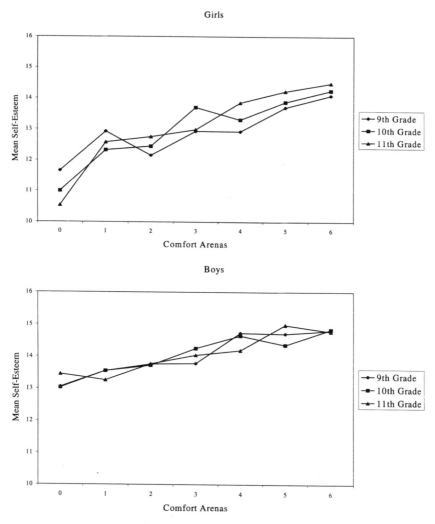

FIG. 4.1. Comfort index and self-esteem.

(see Fig. 4.2). A rather similar pattern for girls and boys is also evident for the association of comfort and well-being (Fig. 4.3).

Turning to depressive mood state, Fig. 4.4 shows that girls' depressive affect decreases monotonically with the proportion of comfort arenas. That is, as girls report more social support across contexts, their depressive affect decreases. For boys, depressed mood shows little variation across the comfort index categories. Differences in the magnitude of the effect are statistically significant each year ($p < .05$). Figure 4.5 demonstrates that girls' tendency to self-derogate is also negatively related to the

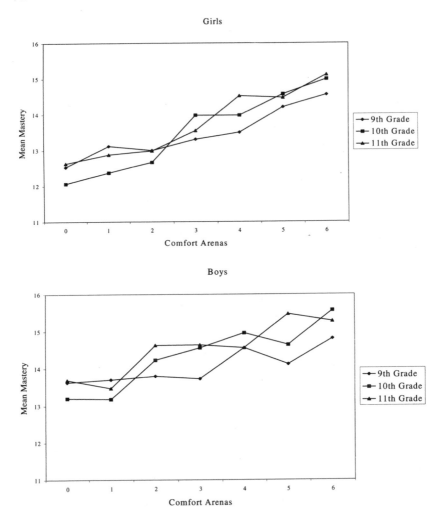

FIG. 4.2.   Comfort index and mastery.

number of arenas in which they find comfort. (Gender differences in effect are statistically significant in Grades 10 and 11; $p < .05$ and $p < .001$, respectively.)

As Fig. 4.1 to Fig. 4.5 illustrate, boys and girls who report multiple comfort arenas are rather comparable with respect to the observed indicators of mental health. However, girls who have few sources of comfort are especially vulnerable to depressive affect, self-derogating cognitions, and low self-esteem. The weakest associations with comfort are found in the realm of achievement. In fact, differences in GPA, by the proportion of comfort arenas, are slight (Fig. 4.6), and there are no gender differences in effect.

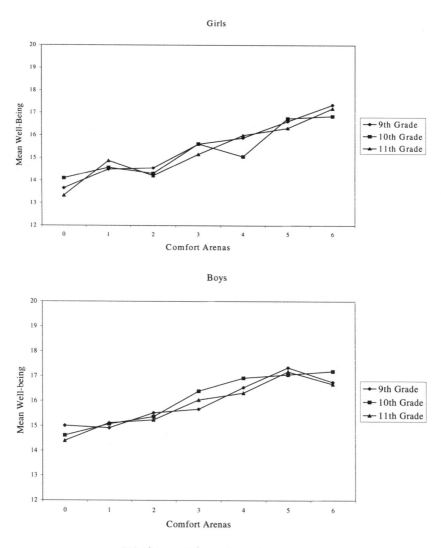

FIG. 4.3.   Comfort index and well-being.

Briefly, as hypothesized, the greater the proportion of arenas the adolescent is comfortable in, the better his or her psychological adjustment. However, the evidence presented thus far suggests that adolescent girls are especially vulnerable to the absence of support in the observed arenas.

Despite the consistent patterns, it is plausible to suppose that these bivariate relations between comfort arenas and developmental outcomes are attributable to uncontrolled factors. Consider self-image as a case in point. If adolescents from higher socioeconomic backgrounds have access

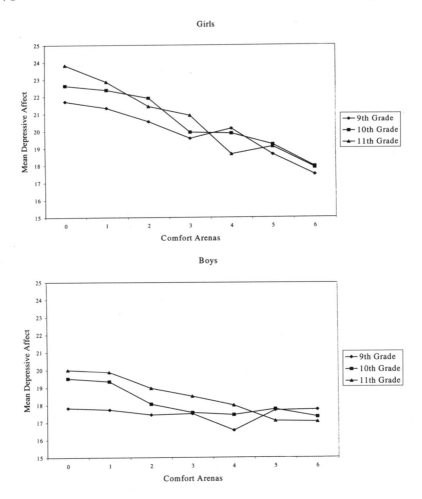

FIG. 4.4.   Comfort index and depressive affect.

to a larger number of comfort arenas, and if more favorable self-images result from relatively abundant economic resources and other advantages
associated with their hierarchical position, any positive observed relationship between the comfort index and self-esteem could be spurious. The
effects of other third variables could likewise render significant bivariate
associations attributable to causal processes other than those presumably
derived from comfort. Therefore, it is necessary to assess the independent
effects of the comfort index on adolescent adjustment, controlling background variables that we have reason to believe contribute to mental
health and school performance (i.e., SES, race, nativity, and family composition).

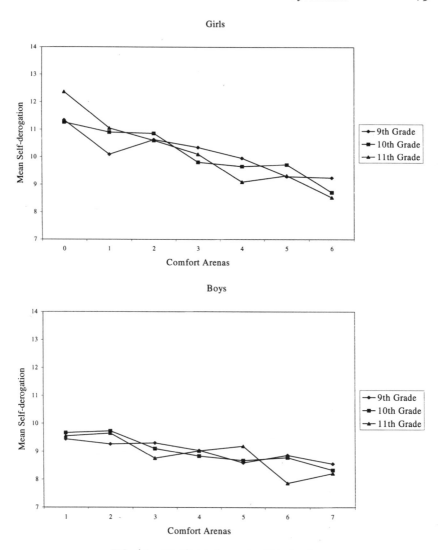

FIG. 4.5.   Comfort index and self-derogation.

It is well established that social disadvantage increases the risk of exposure to negative life events and fosters negative behavioral outcomes (Crockett ,1997; Garmezy, 1985, 1987; Masten & Garmezy, 1985; McLeod & Kessler, 1990; Nettles & Pleck, 1996). Lower SES may even restrict the very number of life arenas that are experienced by the person (Simmons, in press). For example, minority adolescents are less likely than White adolescents to have access to paid employment and therefore to have contacts with mentors in the workplace (Committee on the Health and Safety

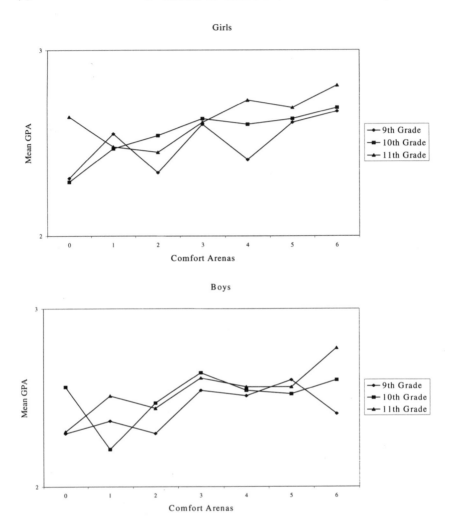

FIG. 4.6.   Comfort index and GPA.

Implications of Child Labor, 1998; Mortimer, 1994; Mortimer, Finch, Dennehy, Lee, & Beebe, 1994).

Furthermore, young people with stronger personal assets (e.g., higher
self-esteem or a stronger sense of mastery) may be able to construct more
satisfying interpersonal relationships, as well as a generally more gratifying life space. In fact, adolescents who are efficacious and have a positive
self-image have been found to select work settings that foster these perceptions (Finch et al., 1991). Similarly, youth with high self-esteem and

high self-efficacy may be better able to evoke positive responses from others and thereby construct experiences that are comforting, provide reinforcing feedback, and promote good self-feelings (Simmons, in press).

Young people who have a generally more positive outlook might also have a tendency to describe their relationships in the contexts of the family, peer group, school, and workplace more favorably and depict themselves in a more auspicious light. In an attempt to distinguish between contexts that create or establish (rather than simply reflect) earlier mental health and achievement, prior indicators of psychological functioning and grades are controlled in the analyses to be presented. That is, to take into account such processes of selection and response set, the 1-year lagged outcome variables are added to the background controls in ordinary least squares regression analyses. Significant effects of comfort may then be more convincingly interpreted as indicating that comfort produces change in the outcomes over time.

The effects of comfort across multiple arenas, net of these controls, are assessed in the 10th and 11th grades only. (Given the absence of a 1-year lagged outcome prior to the ninth grade, our analysis is limited to these years.) To systematically assess gender differences, interaction terms (the product of gender and the comfort index) were introduced one at a time into the equations. Consistent with the bivariate associations, the majority of the interaction terms were found to be statistically significant (i.e., $p <$ .05 in 12 of 18 interactions examined). Therefore, only the gender-specific analyses are presented here.

As shown in Table 4.7, there are clear benefits for adolescents who have multiple sources of comfort. Girls and boys who have a larger proportion of comfort arenas report a stronger sense of well-being, a more positive self-concept (as measured by indexes of self-derogation, self-esteem, and mastery), and lower levels of depressed mood (excepting boys in Grade 10). The proportion of comfort arenas also appears to be a more powerful predictor of psychological adjustment for girls than for boys. The unstandardized beta coefficients, representing the relationship between comfort and the mental health outcomes, tend to be larger for girls than for boys. However, the arenas of comfort index bear no relation to either girls' or boys' academic performance.

In summary, both the bivariate and multivariate analyses show that being comfortable in multiple role relationships, with access to positive interpersonal relationships and social support, is beneficial for adolescents' psychological adjustment. It could be argued, however, that cumulative comfort is inextricably intertwined with the particular sources of comfort that, in fact, constitute the comfort index. For example, if comfort in the family setting were the key variable of importance, and those youth who

TABLE 4.7
Effects of the Comfort Index on Adolescent Adjustment[a]

| Girls | 10th Grade | | 11th Grade | |
Adjustment Outcomes	β	beta	β	beta
Grade point average	.023	.055	.027	.068
Well-being	.395	.246***	.394	.250***
Self-derogation	−.225	−.168***	−.207	−.143***
Self-esteem	.262	.193***	.313	.238***
Depressive affect	−.621	−.203***	−.588	−.186***
Mastery	.396	.287***	.195	.145**
N	(ranges 440–457)		(ranges 421–453)	

| Boys | 10th Grade | | 11th Grade | |
Adjustment Outcomes	β	beta	β	beta
Grade point average	.015	.034	.025	.057
Well-being	.361	.214***	.261	.163**
Self-derogation	−.158	−.114*	−.155	−.108*
Self-esteem	.199	.154**	.205	.149**
Depressive affect	−.272	−.092	−.503	−.165***
Mastery	.254	.194***	.168	.120**
N	(ranges 389–400)		(ranges 371–393)	

Note.   [a]Controlling socioeconomic status, race, nativity, family composition, and scores on prior adjustment measures.
*$p < .05$. **$p < .01$. ***$p < .001$.

experienced comfort in the family also tended to have high scores on the index, then cumulative comfort would not have greater explanatory power than the single sources of comfort considered separately.

To address this possibility, we conducted a series of stepwise regressions, entering in the first step one single source of comfort and the control variables (background and lagged criterion). In the second stage, the cumulative index of comfort was added. The significance of differences in variance explained (R squared) was then assessed by means of an incremental F test. This procedure was conducted separately for boys and girls in each grade (10 and 11) and was repeated for each of the four comfort arenas and all six dependent variables. The results of these analyses (shown in Tables 4.8 and 4.9) provide convincing support for the contention that cumulative comfort, over and above that found in any particular arenas, has a positive effect on adolescent mental health. Indeed, 80 incremental tests of the mental health criteria (4 arenas of comfort times 5 mental health dimensions times 2 genders times 2 grades) yielded just 15 nonsignificant increments ($p > .05$) to the variance explained. Only 2 of

TABLE 4.8
Effects of Single Sources of Comfort as Compared to Cumulative Comfort Index Among 10th Graders

| | Girls | | | | Boys | | | |
| | R^2 | | | | R^2 | | | |
	One Source of Comfort	One Source Plus Index	Degrees of Freedom	p	One Source of Comfort	One Source Plus Index	Degrees of Freedom	p
Family comfort								
Well-being	0.169	0.205	447	< .01	0.150	0.156	382	ns
Self-derogation	0.336	0.354	430	< .01	0.242	0.254	383	< .05
Self-esteem	0.347	0.370	439	< .01	0.152	0.157	390	ns
Depressive affect	0.224	0.239	441	< .01	0.147	0.150	385	ns
Mastery	0.297	0.336	436	< .01	0.238	0.255	381	< .01
Grade point average	0.436	0.436	432	ns	0.386	0.386	379	ns
Peer comfort								
Well-being	0.163	0.208	405	< .01	0.126	0.155	345	< .01
Self-derogation	0.388	0.399	386	< .01	0.243	0.249	344	ns
Self-esteem	0.346	0.368	395	< .01	0.127	.0137	351	< .05
Depressive affect	0.207	0.230	399	< .01	0.149	0.155	347	ns
Mastery	0.331	0.374	395	< .01	0.238	0.255	346	< .01
Grade point average	0.429	0.432	390	ns	0.386	0.390	340	ns

(Continued)

TABLE 4.8
(Continued)

	Girls				Boys			
	R^2				R^2			
	One Source of Comfort	One Source Plus Index	Degrees of Freedom	p	One Source of Comfort	One Source Plus Index	Degrees of Freedom	p
Work comfort								
Well-being	0.226	0.271	184	< .01	0.100	.0157	147	< .01
Self-derogation	0.239	0.251	174	ns	0.261	0.266	146	ns
Self-esteem	0.330	0.351	183	< .05	0.150	0.166	149	ns
Depressive affect	0.157	0.205	183	< .01	0.111	0.111	146	ns
Mastery	0.253	0.314	179	< .01	0.170	0.196	146	< .05
Grade point average	0.337	0.340	176	ns	0.334	0.355	143	ns
School Comfort								
Well-being	0.180	0.206	444	< .01	0.132	0.167	373	< .01
Self-derogation	0.349	0.360	427	< .01	0.249	0.254	375	ns
Self-esteem	0.351	0.366	436	< .01	0.166	0.183	382	< .01
Depressive affect	0.212	0.235	438	< .01	0.142	0.147	376	ns
Mastery	0.300	0.337	433	< .01	0.243	0.266	373	< .01
Grade point average	0.427	0.431	432	ns	0.382	0.382	379	ns

TABLE 4.9
Effects of Single Sources of Comfort as Compared to Cumulative Comfort Index Among 11th Graders

	Girls				Boys			
	R^2				R^2			
	One Source of Comfort	One Source Plus Index	Degrees of Freedom	p	One Source of Comfort	One Source Plus Index	Degrees of Freedom	p
Family comfort								
Well-being	0.223	0.265	436	< .01	0.193	0.208	376	< .01
Self-derogation	0.440	0.445	429	< .05	0.319	0.330	376	< .05
Self-esteem	0.377	0.398	437	< .01	0.224	0.245	382	< .01
Depressive affect	0.245	0.270	436	< .01	0.263	0.274	380	< .05
Mastery	0.292	0.299	429	< .05	0.270	0.282	376	< .05
Grade point average	0.393	0.400	411	< .05	0.405	0.407	360	ns
Peer comfort								
Well-being	0.259	0.280	439	< .01	0.188	0.204	376	< .01
Self-derogation	0.492	0.439	432	< .01	0.323	0.330	373	< .05
Self-esteem	0.362	0.390	440	< .01	0.234	0.250	379	< .01
Depressive affect	0.258	0.271	439	< .01	0.242	0.261	378	< .01
Mastery	0.290	0.296	431	ns	0.267	0.276	374	< .05
Grade point average	0.399	0.403	408	ns	0.403	0.405	357	ns

(Continued)

81

TABLE 4.9
(Continued)

	Girls				Boys			
	R^2				R^2			
	One Source of Comfort	One Source Plus Index	Degrees of Freedom	p	One Source of Comfort	One Source Plus Index	Degrees of Freedom	p
Work comfort								
Well-being	0.252	0.293	262	< .01	0.146	0.164	198	< .05
Self-derogation	0.513	0.526	258	< .01	0.334	0.341	199	ns
Self-esteem	0.401	0.444	261	< .01	0.232	0.234	204	ns
Depressive affect	0.311	0.353	263	< .01	0.277	0.289	201	ns
Mastery	0.336	0.365	256	< .01	0.244	0.259	200	< .05
Grade point average	0.386	0.391	253	ns	0.369	0.369	198	ns
School Comfort								
Well-being	0.241	0.281	420	< .01	0.188	0.204	356	< .01
Self-derogation	0.446	0.462	412	< .01	0.343	0.352	355	< .05
Self-esteem	0.375	0.417	420	< .01	0.217	0.242	360	< .01
Depressive affect	0.279	0.296	419	< .01	0.249	0.283	358	< .01
Mastery	0.285	0.303	411	< .01	0.279	0.287	356	< .05
Grade point average	0.403	0.404	413	ns	0.410	0.413	363	ns

these occurred among the girls and 13 for the boys. The general pattern observed earlier is confirmed: Cumulative comfort matters for adolescent mental health, and it appears to be even more important for girls than it is for boys. However, consistent with the results using ANOVA, only 1 of 16 incremental tests for GPA (among 11th-grade girls) demonstrated a significant difference in the amount of variance explained.

THE INFLUENCE OF EACH COMFORT ARENA ON ADJUSTMENT

Now that we have shown that cumulative comfort matters, we turn to the question of whether some contexts are more consequential or protective than others. It may be that particular sources of comfort are especially critical for adolescent adjustment. The consequences of comfort in the various arenas could also change as adolescents grow older, although the restriction of our observations to a 2-year period limits assessment of such developmental changes. In the analyses to follow, comfort in each arena (family, peers, school, and work) is expressed by a dummy variable signifying social support, coded 1 if comfortable (as indicated by criteria described in chap. 2). As before, to avoid spurious findings, the mental health and achievement outcomes are regressed on the comfort indicators, controlling background variables, gender, and the lagged outcomes (indicating prior levels of adjustment).

Separation of workers and nonworkers is necessitated by the fact that they have different opportunities for comfort. Workers have four such arenas (family, peers, school, and work), the nonworkers only three. However, analyses by work status have a further advantage in that they enable us to examine differences between employed and nonemployed adolescents in the consequences of comfort.

That is, it is reasonable to suppose that employment would affect comfort dynamics in the family, with friends, and at school. Employed adolescents are operating in a domain that will be crucially important to them as adults. Because most adolescents anticipate that they will be invested in the work role through their adult lives, functioning in this domain may be seen, by the workers themselves as well as their parents and other significant others, as movement toward maturity and responsibility. Several adultlike attitudes and behaviors may be expected to result from this new-found status. For example, if employed adolescents become more independent of their families (Aronson, Mortimer, Zierman, & Hacker, 1996; Mortimer & Shanahan, 1994; Phillips & Sandstrom, 1990), parent–child relationships may be less consequential for the mental health of working adolescents. Growing financial independence could be accompanied by increased emotional independence.

Moreover, there is evidence that adolescents who are initially less strongly engaged in school (as measured in the ninth grade) work longer hours during high school (Mortimer & Johnson, 1998; Steinberg & Avenevoli, 1998). If working adolescents are less involved with, and obtain less gratification from, educational pursuits, support from teachers may be less important for them and less consequential for their psychological health. In contrast, adolescents who are initially more oriented to their peers work more intensively during high school. The increased salience of peers could make support from a friend particularly consequential for employed students' self-image and mental health.

A preliminary analysis examined whether each of the four comfort arenas would have different implications for boys and for girls. A series of equations included the comfort arenas, background variables, lagged variables, gender, and terms reflecting the interaction of gender with each comfort arena entered one at a time. Of 84 such interaction terms, only 4 were found to be statistically significant. Because such a small number of significant interactions could have occurred by chance, we do not present separate analyses by gender. It seems rather paradoxical to find that cumulative comfort should be more important for girls than boys, but that each single source of comfort does not interact with gender to influence mental health. Does this provide further indication that diverse sources of comfort, experienced in tandem, are what make a difference, particularly for girls?

Let us first consider nonworking 10th-grade adolescents' achievement and mental health. Table 4.10 shows pervasive psychological impacts of comfort with parents. That is, those 10th graders who enjoy supportive relationships with their parents exhibit higher well-being, self-esteem, and mastery and are less likely to manifest self-derogation or depressive affect. Comfort with a friend is likewise consequential for four of the five mental health outcomes. The degree of comfort with teachers affects only one outcome—the sense of mastery. Interestingly, as in the case of the cumulative measure of comfort, none of the particular domains of comfort manifest significant effects on grade point average.

In view of the high degree of stability of these mental health indicators, these analyses are rather stringent. They show rather convincingly that comfort, and especially comfort with parents and friends, is important for nonworking adolescents' psychological health. Including gender in the equation controls, boys' purported mental health advantages—higher well-being, self-esteem, and mastery, and lesser tendencies toward depressive affect and self-derogation—are not always empirically demonstrated. It is somewhat surprising to find that the indicators of advantage

TABLE 4.10

Influence of Each Comfort Arena on Adjustment, Nonemployed 10th-Grade Adolescents

Variables	Grade Point Average		Well-Being		Self-Derogation		Self-Esteem		Depressive Affect		Mastery	
	β	beta	β	beta	β	beta	β	beta	β	beta	β	beta
Comfort with parents	.004	.002	1.383	.213***	-.722	-.129**	.513	.096*	-2.252	-.186***	1.003	.181***
Comfort with a friend	-.053	-.030	.803	.127**	-.653	-.121**	.886	.173***	-.756	-.064	.644	.120**
Comfort with teacher	.103	.060	.492	.079	-.269	-.050	.189	.037	-.723	-.062	.786	.148**
Socioeconomic status	.041	.082	-.042	-.023	-.049	-.032	-.052	-.035	-.260	-.078	.196	.130**
Race	.138	.072	.028	.004	.698	.116**	-.259	-.045	.486	.037	-.191	-.032
Nativity	-.166	-.045	-.033	-.003	-.202	-.018	-.115	-.011	.098	.004	.358	.032
Family composition	.012	.007	.457	.068	-.036	-.006	.215	.039	-.105	-.008	.028	.005
Gender	-.016	-.009	1.009	.162**	-.681	-.128***	.856	.169***	-1.522	-.131**	1.008	.191***
Prior adjustment	.632	.619***	.306	.295***	.553	.542***	.501	.492***	.431	.412***	.418	.395***
R^2	.455***		.231***		.422***		.375***		.292***		.356***	
Number of cases	382		383		377		383		382		380	

Note. *p < .05. **p < .01. ***p < .001.

and disadvantage—SES, race, nativity, and family composition—have such minimal effects. However, if enduring features of social background have influenced mental health at earlier stages of the life course, prior to the ninth grade, these would be captured in the lagged outcome variables. Tests of the effects of the social background variables in this analysis could then be quite conservative. (This could also hold for our tests of the comfort variables to the extent that they also have long-term and rather stable influence.)

Turning to the employed 10th graders (Table 4.11), we find a generally weaker pattern of significant relations (and lower R square values across dependent variables). Comfort with parents significantly influences only two of the five mental health dimensions. Thus, adolescents who are employed in the 10th grade seem to be less responsive to the quality of parent–child relations, in terms of their mental health, than those who are not employed. Comfort with parents does, however, show a positive effect on working adolescents' GPA. Contrary to our speculations about the greater salience of peers for working teenagers, comfort with friends influences only two of the five mental health dimensions.

Comfort at school bears a significant relation to only one outcome—well-being. It is noteworthy that comfort at school has such limited influence for both groups. As shown in chapter 3, adolescents typically report comfortable relationships with teachers. However, these relations may be sufficiently impersonal and transient so as to have limited impact on adolescent mental health.

As displayed in Table 4.12, comfort with parents continues to exhibit pervasive effects on the mental health of nonemployed 11th-grade adolescents, significantly affecting their well-being, self-derogation, self-esteem, and depressive affect. Comfort with friends positively impacts their well-being. None of the comfort-related measures is significantly related to academic achievement.

Comparing the nonworking and working 11th graders (coefficients for the latter are shown in Table 4.13), we find that comfort with parents is somewhat less important among the workers, significantly influencing three of the five dimensions (self-esteem, depressive affect, and mastery). Comparison of peer influence in the two groups is now consistent with our prior formulation. That is, comfort with friends influences all five mental health dimensions among the 11th-grade workers, but only one among the nonemployed 11th graders (Table 4.12). Comfort with parents may be receding as a determinant of mental health; at the same time, comfort with friends is coming to have a more pronounced effect. For the employed students, comfort at school positively influences well-being; comfort at work has a positive impact on self-esteem and a negative effect on depressed mood. Again, the lagged outcomes are highly predictive of future mental health states as well as achievement.

TABLE 4.11
Influence of Each Comfort Arena on Adjustment, Employed 10th-Grade Adolescents

Variables	Grade Point Average		Well-Being		Self-Derogation		Self-Esteem		Depressive Affect		Mastery	
	β	beta	β	beta	β	beta	β	beta	β	beta	β	beta
Comfort with parents	.198	.125*	.795	.126*	.247	.045	.366	.069	-.368	-.030	.589	.108*
Comfort with a friend	-.129	-.084	.752	.122*	-.305	-.056	.300	.058	-.451	-.038	.634	.119*
Comfort with teacher	-.021	-.014	.739	.123*	-.482	-.090	.484	.095	-1.283	-.110	.333	.064
Comfort at work	-.001	-.001	.063	.010	-.118	-.022	.021	.004	.042	.004	.188	.036
Socioeconomic status	.015	.030	-.092	-.048	-.040	-.024	.040	.025	-.091	-.024	.088	.052
Race	.028	.015	.349	.044	.305	.044	-.334	-.051	.859	.056	-.252	-.036
Nativity	-.241	-.086	.438	.038	-.919	-.090	.691	.074	-1.444	-.065	.391	.039
Family composition	.017	.010	.235	.035	-.291	-.049	.566	.100	.378	.029	.029	.005
Gender	-.031	-.021	.790	.131*	-.641	-.121*	.414	.081	-.873	-.075	.421	.081
Prior adjustment	.494	.494***	.294	.296***	.534	.476***	.482	.430***	.352	.341***	.513	.460***
R^2	.314***		.198***		.287***		.274***		.167***		.302***	
Number of cases	298		306		292		303		304		299	

Note. $*p < .05.$ $**p < .01.$ $***p < .001.$

TABLE 4.12

Influence of Each Comfort Arena on Adjustment, Nonemployed 11th-Grade Adolescents

Variables	Grade Point Average		Well-Being		Self-Derogation		Self-Esteem		Depressive Affect		Mastery	
	β	beta	β	beta	β	beta	β	beta	β	beta	β	beta
Comfort with parents	-.033	-.021	.906	.154**	-.651	-.120*	.821	.158**	-1.196	-.104*	.347	.067
Comfort with a friend	.033	.021	.637	.108*	-.086	-.016	.412	.079	-.446	-.039	.102	.020
Comfort with teacher	.059	.038	.058	.010	-.395	-.073	.278	.054	.177	.015	.169	.033
Socioeconomic status	.088	.211***	.078	.051	-.105	-.075	.120	.089	-.357	-.119*	.126	.095
Race	.030	.018	-.974	-.158**	.745	.131*	-.821	-.151**	1.088	.090	-.527	-.097
Nativity	-.096	-.034	1.349	.128*	-.294	-.029	.750	.081	-.909	-.043	1.502	.164**
Family composition	-.028	-.018	-.340	-.057	.805	.148**	-.369	-.070	1.333	.115*	-.550	-.106*
Gender	-.082	-.053	.174	.031	.017	.003	.248	.049	-.424	-.038	.448	.089
Prior adjustment	.531	.545***	.380	.427***	.561	.558***	.454	.460***	.502	.467***	.436	.433***
R^2	.448***		.298***		.400***		.326***		.275***		.293***	
Number of cases	297		302		297		302		300		297	

Note. *$p < .05$. **$p < .01$. ***$p < .001$.

TABLE 4.13

Influence of Each Comfort Arena on Adjustment, Employed 11th-Grade Adolescents

Variables	Grade Point Average β	beta	Well-Being β	beta	Self-Derogation β	beta	Self-Esteem β	beta	Depressive Affect β	beta	Mastery β	beta
Comfort with parents	.040	.024	.429	.069	-.393	-.068	.482	.092*	-1.213	-.100*	.477	.089*
Comfort with a friend	-.009	-.005	.715	.114*	-.767	-.132**	.635	.120**	-1.831	-.149**	.715	.132**
Comfort with teacher	.071	.045	.561	.094*	.066	.012	.239	.048	-.852	-.073	.324	.063
Comfort at work	.050	.032	.491	.083	-.232	-.042	.653	.131**	-.962	-.083*	.123	.024
Socioeconomic status	.074	.146***	.032	.017	.050	.028	.049	.030	.159	.042	.000	.000
Race	.204	.102*	.202	.026	-.786	-.110**	.168	.026	-.982	-.065	.589	.088*
Nativity	-.093	-.028	.315	.025	.634	.054	.453	.043	-.771	-.031	.693	.063
Family composition	.203	.121**	.319	.050	.012	.002	.249	.046	-.424	-.034	.290	.053
Gender	-.094	-.060	.592	.099*	-.789	-.143***	.548	.109**	-1.626	-.139***	.501	.098*
Prior adjustment	.524	.502***	.351	.356***	.648	.618***	.509	.502***	.444	.442***	.464	.463***
R^2	.381***		.214***		.470***		.364***		.308***		.328***	
Number of cases	459		455		450		458		458		450	

Note. *$p < .05$. **$p < .01$. ***$p < .001$.

Considering the results as a whole, comfortable relationships in the family are repeatedly found to be the most consequential to adolescents' mental health. Support from friends affects adolescents' adjustment to a lesser extent. Given the structural barriers to establishing close and meaningful relationships with teachers in today's high schools, it is perhaps not surprising that comfort at school exerts so little influence on adolescents' psychological adjustment. Comfort at work, with supervisors or coworkers, begins to exert significant influence on the mental health of working teens in the 11th grade.

As noted earlier, social background shows relatively little influence in these analyses, but the long-term character of these influences, coupled with the stability of the mental health and achievement dimensions, suggests caution in our interpretation of the findings.

Comparisons by year and work status are somewhat perilous. That is, the composition of working and nonworking subgroups changes across time due to the considerable movement of adolescents in and out of the labor force. Still there is evidence that support in the family arena is consistently more important for nonemployed adolescents' mental health. Comfort with friends becomes especially important as a source of psychological health for working adolescents in the 11th grade. It is interesting to find that comfort at work has an independent additive effect net of the other comfort sources on 11th-grade workers' self-esteem and depressive affect.

SUMMARY AND CONCLUSIONS

Simmons (in press; Simmons & Blyth, 1987) emphasized the problems inherent in the total absence of an arena of comfort. However, only a minority of adolescents lack comfort in all four domains (family, peers, school, and work). Therefore, we examined whether adolescents who have more arenas of comfort are more advantaged than those with fewer. The initial analyses presented in this chapter support the conclusion that adolescents who have access to a greater number of arenas of comfort manifest better mental health. Consistent with research on adult subjects (Wethington & Kessler, 1986), it appears that supportive relations across a number of domains are likewise more consequential for adolescent girls than for boys. The significance of comfort, and its stronger predictive power for girls, was shown across adjustment outcomes and in both bivariate and multivariate analyses. As previously suggested, the fact that the latter control for the 1-year lagged mental health dimensions makes these analyses particularly stringent. Given the long-term stability of both comfort and the mental health outcomes across time, it could be argued that our analyses are all too conservative; that is, comfort may be even more consequential than our analyses indicate if the self-image and other mental health variables have already been subject to the influence of positive relationships in these various domains. However, Simmons (in press; Simmons & Blyth, 1987) was especially concerned with the contemporaneous experience of comfort in adolescence—a stage of life in which numerous changes are occurring and support across multiple domains may be particularly important. Given our central purpose, to subject Simmons' hypotheses to empirical test, it would appear that the analyses we conducted are appropriate.

Second, this chapter addressed the independent effects of comfort in each of four arenas in an attempt to understand whether having supportive relationships in certain domains is more important than in others. Although pitting one source of comfort against another may be questioned in view of their supposed positive relations to one another, they actually bear rather little empirical association (their relations are further assessed in chap. 5). The multivariate analyses showed that supportive relationships with parents were more consequential to adolescents' mental health than supportive, comfortable relationships with friends, at school, and at work. These results certainly coincide with prior research emphasizing the continued salience of family relations even as the adolescent seeks autonomy and independence at this time of life (Galambos & Ehrenberg, 1997; Gecas & Seff, 1991; Jessor & Jessor, 1977; LeCroy, 1989; Maccoby & Martin, 1983; Mortimer et al., 1986; Steinberg & Silverberg, 1986).

Third, we tested the hypothesis that employed adolescents would be less responsive to the influence of parent–child relationships and therefore also less vulnerable when these relationships are not supportive. Our comparative analyses, enabling inspection of the effects of comfort in working and nonworking subgroups, showed support for this hypothesis in both the 10th and 11th grades. Moreover, the mental health of 11th-grade employed adolescents was found to be more responsive to positive peer relationships than that of 11th graders who were not working. Whereas some commentators have expressed concern that working adolescents may grow up too quickly, taking on an adultlike identity too soon (Greenberger & Steinberg, 1986), it should be noted that acquiring a degree of emotional independence from parents is a normal developmental task at this time of life. Apparently having a job promotes this state of mind. Although orientation to peers may not always be a good thing, much would appear to hinge on the quality of relationships with those peers and the extent to which peers promote achievement-oriented values and goals, or less salutary, nonconforming attitudes and behaviors.

We find that academic achievement is not responsive to comfort dynamics at least given our measurement of these influences. Virtually no relation was found between grades and comfort, whether measured cumulatively or in terms of the separate domains. Comfort with parents was found to have a positive effect on GPA in only one group—employed 10th graders. None of the other comfort measures had significant impact on school performance.

As for the social background variables, they are generally found to have rather circumscribed effects that are inconsistent across grade and subgroup. For example, socioeconomic background had a positive influence on grades among the 11th but not the 10th graders. It may be that at this stage of life, ascribed characteristics come to assume less importance for adolescents' mental health than their own achievements.

In chapter 5, we turn to a key proposition in Simmons' (in press; Simmons & Blyth, 1987) formulation: Comfortable relationships and experiences in one sphere can buffer the adverse effects of change and discomfort in other spheres. We examine this proposition by considering whether comfort with friends, at school, or at work can buffer the otherwise deleterious consequences of change and strained, uncomfortable relationships with parents for an adolescent's achievement and psychological functioning.

CHAPTER FIVE

Arenas of Comfort
as Stress Moderators

Yet to be evaluated are the interrelations of arenas of comfort and discomfort in the production of psychological and behavioral outcomes. Simmons and Blyth (1987) hypothesized that the presence of an arena of comfort within the life space provides opportunity for the individual to relax and rejuvenate so that problematic events and experiences elsewhere can be endured or overcome. They thought that positive social relationships and experiences in one domain could soothe the person and compensate for experiences that are threatening to the self-image in other life spheres. The findings presented in this chapter provide evidence that the presence of an extrafamilial arena of comfort does, in fact, condition the effects of change and/or discomfort in the family sphere.

The family was selected as the analytic context for change events and discomfort because it is probably the arena of greatest long-term exposure and commitment for adolescents. Furthermore, change and discomfort in the family are highly salient to adolescents and often disturbing (Eccles et al., 1997; Gecas & Seff, 1991; Hetherington, 1989; Jessor & Jessor, 1977; LeCroy, 1989; Maccoby & Martin, 1983).

The family is traditionally thought of as a safe haven, a place where one is able to find solace from daily challenges and difficulties (Lasch, 1977). However, home is not necessarily an arena of comfort for an adolescent whose family is undergoing change or at times when relationships with parents are fraught with discord. During adolescence, disengagement from parents is the normal course of events; adolescents typically strive for autonomy and explore new identities outside the family sphere (Csikszentmihalyi & Larson, 1984; Galambos & Ehrenberg, 1997; Steinberg, 1990). As the home becomes a less comfortable environment, peer, school, or work contexts may become more comfortable, concordant with this stage-specific growth and self-actualization process.

Although some tension between adolescents and their parents is to be anticipated, given changing expectations on each side about appropriate levels of autonomy and behavioral limits (Brooks-Gunn, 1991; Smetana et al., 1991), chronic strain in the parent–adolescent relationship has clear developmental costs. Uncomfortable, unsupportive relationships with parents have been shown to have wide-ranging detrimental outcomes, including problem behavior (Jessor & Jessor, 1977; LeCroy, 1989), negative self-concept (Gecas & Seff, 1991; Mortimer et al., 1986), diminished psychological health and academic performance (Maccoby & Martin, 1983), low self-reliance, and other indicators of responsible independence (Steinberg & Silverberg, 1986). Evidence that problems with parents have pervasive negative impacts holds across a broad spectrum of socioeconomic and ethnic groups.

Parent–adolescent relationships characterized by a lack of communication and affection may be considered ongoing proximal stressors (Cohen & Wills, 1985; Wheaton, 1990). Such daily hassles are subjectively experienced as persistent strains in the immediate environment (Cohen & Wills, 1985; Compas, Davis, Forsythe, & Wagner, 1986; Delongis et al., 1982; Rowlinson & Felner, 1988). Stressors may also take the form of discrete, acute events, such as the loss of a job or parental divorce. Research on adults (Delongis et al., 1982) and adolescents (Compas, Davis, Forsythe, & Wagner, 1986; Rowlinson & Felner, 1988) suggests that daily stressors may be even more detrimental to individual functioning than major life events.

Studies of stress buffering during adolescence typically examine social support (from friends and family) as moderators of the effects of life events (Windle, 1992). The results of this research are mixed (Compas, 1987; Windle, 1992). Inconsistencies in the findings may be partially attributed to the failure to consider the ecology of stress and coping processes. That is, support may be more effective if it comes from outside the immediate stressor context. For example, in Lepore's (1992) sample of college students, support from a close friend moderated the psychological distress associated with frequent conflict with a roommate.

Involvement with friends, school, and other activities may be particularly important for adolescents whose relationships with parents are distant and lacking in support (Galambos & Ehrenberg, 1997; Savin-Williams & Berndt, 1990) or whose parents are divorcing or remarrying (Hetherington, 1989). Gratifying activities and accomplishments in these settings could strengthen personal resources (i.e., self-esteem and self-efficacy) and moderate the disturbances brought on by change and discomfort at home (Bandura, 1986; Rutter, 1990). In addition to the immediate benefits derived from support outside the family, the skills, values, and self-knowledge developed at school and work could have enduring consequences for the adolescent's mental health and adaptive potential (Csikszentmihalyi &

Larson, 1984; Mortimer & Finch, 1996). The compensating effects of experiences at work could be especially important to adolescents who are not comfortable or engaged in school (Elliott & Voss, 1974).

The study of intercontextual processes, or *mesosystem* interrelations (Bronfenbrenner, 1979, 1986), is typically focused on adults' work and family linkages (Bielby, 1992)—specifically, how workplace stressors spill over into the family (Galambos, Sears, Almeida, & Kolaric, 1995). Sometimes the adverse consequences of problems encountered in the workplace are alleviated by spouse support (Pearlin & McCall, 1990; Weiss, 1990). However, if work stress diminishes support from others at home, the worker is placed at even greater risk for poor adjustment (Liem & Liem, 1990).

Consideration of the implications that positive work experiences might have for family life is much less common. Piotrkowski and Crits-Christoph (1981) suggested that, for some women, satisfying psychological states and cognitions with respect to work (i.e., positive job mood, intrinsic job gratification, job security, and job satisfaction) have salutary effects on their relationships with family members and their mood at home. The possibility that work experiences and supports act to moderate or condition the psychological impacts of family stress for adults has been given little attention. However, some research (Kandel et al., 1985; Wheaton, 1990) indicates that a woman's employment can buffer the negative consequences of marital problems.

Similar intercontextual and interpersonal dynamics could likewise occur in adolescence. Can supportive, positive relationships with friends, teachers, supervisors, or coworkers moderate major changes that occur at home, or strained relationships with parents? Can accomplishments and engagement in school and/or work, and the satisfactions derived therefrom, diminish or offset difficulties at home, compensating for the lack of positive feedback from parents? Might such involvement distract the adolescent from negative ruminations about relationships and events in the family arena? Alternatively, if school or work is stressful or uncomfortable for the adolescent, will these experiences intensify the negative consequences of family change and discord?

MODEL OF ADOLESCENT STRESS
AND THE MODERATING EFFECTS
OF ARENAS OF COMFORT

This chapter assesses both acute, eventlike stressors and ongoing proximal strains in the family context. Although the adolescent could retreat to a number of potential arenas when circumstances and relations in the family are stressful, this analysis is restricted to three extrafamilial settings:

the peer group, school, and workplace. In addition to the moderating power of social support, the buffering effects of other experiences in the school and work domains (i.e., the full set of comfort measures, listed in Appendix B) are explored.

According to our conceptual model of adolescent stress, shown in Fig. 5.1, objective change in the family (the change context in this analysis) fosters discomfort (Path A); discomfort, in turn, jeopardizes mental health and achievement (Path B). Family change also has direct negative effects on the adolescent adjustment (Path E). Each comfort arena outside the family (peers, school, and work) is also expected to be consequential for adolescent adjustment.

The moderating effects of comfort in the peer relationship, school context, and work setting are of central interest (Paths C, D, and F) given the growing significance of activities within these domains during adolescence. Conditional relationships are explored using regression with interaction terms (Paths B, D, E, and F are estimated using OLS regression; lo-

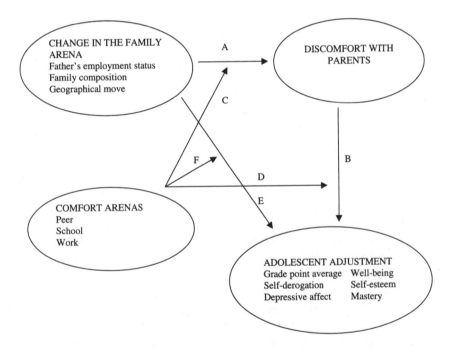

Note. All equations control socioeconomic status, race, nativity, gender, and scores on prior adjustment measures.

FIG. 5.1.   Model of adolescent stress and the moderating effects of arenas of comfort.

gistic regression is used to explore Paths A and C because the dependent variable—discomfort in the family—is dichotomous). Significant interaction terms indicate the presence of a buffering effect.

Thus, family change (Path E), comfort in one of the proposed comfort domains (path not shown), and the interaction between family change and comfort outside the family (Path F) predict adolescent mental health and achievement. Discomfort in the family context (Path B), comfort in one of the proposed comfort domains (path not shown), and the interaction between family discomfort and the extrafamilial arena of comfort (Path D) are additional predictors of the key adjustment outcomes. (To simplify the figure and because comfort in all nonfamily arenas is not included in the conditional analyses featured in this chapter, paths representing the direct effects of the extrafamilial arenas on discomfort with parents and on adolescent adjustment are not shown.)

Although the arena of comfort hypothesis is centrally concerned with psychological adjustment under stressful conditions, it can be fruitfully extended to comfort itself—to the quality of one's experience in a particular setting. For example, the presence of supportive relationships and satisfying experiences in extrafamily arenas could directly ameliorate the disruptions and pressures on the parent–adolescent relationship, induced by change events in the family (Path C). The absence of such extrafamily comfort could, in contrast, exacerbate the relational problems accompanying family change. When adolescents do not experience comfort and support outside their families, they may become more emotionally dependent on their parents. A heavy demand on the parent–adolescent relationship, at a time when disengagement from parents is the statistically normal as well as socially normative developmental course, could make the quality of family life more vulnerable to stressors generated from change in the family. It is also possible that comfort in extrafamilial domains would have direct effects on family discomfort, and these need to be controlled in assessing such plausible conditional relations.

Therefore, change in the family context (Path A), comfort in one of the proposed extrafamilial comfort arenas—for example, comfort in the peer, school, and work domains (path not shown)—and the interaction between family change and comfort in the moderating arena (Path C) under scrutiny predict discomfort in the family.

The analyses are performed for the total sample, controlling all background variables included in prior analyses and the 1-year lagged outcome variable. (Interaction analyses were performed on all paths of interest in Fig. 5.1 to examine whether the direct or indirect impact of family change or discomfort on adolescent adjustment, or the moderating influence of extrafamilial comfort, varies for girls and boys. Few interaction terms were significant; therefore the results for the total panel are presented.)

A variety of changes within the family arena between the 9th and 10th grades are considered: change in the father's employment status, change in family composition, and a geographical move by the family or adolescent (i.e., the entire family may move or the adolescent may move away from home).

Change in the father's employment status between the 9th and 10th grades occurred for 4.7% of the adolescents. This could signify a job loss, retirement, or a move into the workforce. Change in family composition (derived from a self-report item that asked the adolescents to list the current members of their households) could reflect many different kinds of transitions. For example, a two-parent intact family could become a single-parent home; the custodial parent could remarry; the adolescent could move in with other relatives, friends, foster parents, and so on. A change of some kind in family composition was reported by 13.3% of the participants. Nearly 17% of the adolescents experienced a geographical move between the 9th and 10th grades. Among the 16.8% who moved, this experience ranged from a move within the city of St. Paul (the majority, 66%, of moves are of this type), from the city to a suburb or beyond (including 21% of all moves), out of state (about 8% of all moves), to outside the United States (approximately 4% of the adolescents who moved).

These measures of change do not incorporate assessment of whether the event is perceived as positive or negative by the adolescent. Thoits (1983, 1991) cogently argued that life events need to be assessed in terms of the personal meaning they hold for the individual. Rutter (1983) pointed out that psychiatric disorders are largely associated with undesirable incidents. However, Luthar (1991) found that, during periods of rapid change such as adolescence, even positive events can lead to the perception that the environment is uncertain and unstable, increasing the adolescent's vulnerability. We therefore include changes in the analyses irrespective of their implied positive or negative subjective quality.

Discomfort in the family arena is indicated by the absence of comfortable relationships with either parent. Adolescents who do not perceive supportive relationships with either parent constitute 33.4% of the 10th graders.

To maximize the size of the panel to be included in these analyses, we utilize data from the first and second years of the study only. Whereas change in the family arena is measured between the 9th and 10th grades, all other constructs are measured in Grade 10. Thus, causal paths from family change to family discomfort and to adolescent adjustment (mental health and achievement) assume a corresponding temporal order. However, consistent with the assumption that the quality of the relationship with parents, as well as experiences in other spheres, have contemporaneous influence, comfort in all arenas and the adolescent adjustment outcomes are measured at the same time—in Grade 10. It is plausible to expect that the currently experienced level of comfort in the family and other arenas would have stronger implications for adolescent adjustment than that experienced a year earlier.

Before examining the findings, it should be noted that the statistical significance of an interaction term depends on the number of adolescents for whom the stressor and the modifying factor (in this case, presence of comfort in an extrafamilial arena) co-occur. Thus, it is quite possible that a true interactive effect would be concealed because it applies to only a small proportion of the sample. This may be especially problematic when examining Paths C and F given the small proportion of adolescents in the panel who experience the particular family changes under investigation between the 9th and 10th grades.

Table 5.1 shows correlations among event stressors (occurrences of change), a lack of comfort in the family (strained parent–adolescent relationships), the mental health and achievement outcomes, and the moderator variables (the full list of comfort indicators in peer, school, and work arenas). The event stressors are found to be associated with several of the criterion variables. For example, a change in the father's employment status co-occurs with more intense self-derogation, more frequent depressive affect, and a weaker sense of mastery. Change in family composition is linked to poorer school performance. Similarly, a geographical move is related to lower grade point average (GPA) and greater depressive affect. Discomfort with parents is significantly related to all six of the outcomes; all correlations are in the expected direction.

When examining interaction effects in the context of regression models, it is recommended that moderators be uncorrelated with both the predictor and outcome variables (Baron & Kenny, 1986; Cronbach, 1987). Table 5.1 demonstrates that several relationships among the moderators, stressors, and adjustment outcomes are significant. However, the strength of these associations is modest ($r < .25$), indicating that the displayed intercorrelations are acceptable for investigating the moderating influence of comfort with friends, at school, and at work.

Direct paths representing the influence of family changes on parent–adolescent discomfort and the effects of both family constructs (i.e., change and discomfort) on adolescent achievement and mental health (i.e., Paths A, B, and E) are estimated without controls for the experience of comfort in extrafamily domains (peers, school, and work). This is because we are more interested in the direct, or modifying, influence of experiences of comfort in particular domains than on knowing whether such effects are independent of experiences in all other comfort arenas. For example, we wish to ascertain whether change or discomfort in the family setting has a significant impact on adjustment (net of social background and lagged

TABLE 5.1

Correlations of 10th-Grade Stressors, Adolescent Adjustment, and Comforts

	1.	2.	3.	4.	5.	6.	7.	8.	9.
1. Father's employment status	1.00								
2. Change in family composition	.05	1.00							
3. Geographical move	.06	.29***	1.00						
4. Discomfort with parents	-.00	-.03	-.05	1.00					
5. Grade point average	-.07	-.13***	-.14***	-.17***	1.00				
6. Well-being	-.04	-.02	-.00	-.35***	.16***	1.00			
7. Self-derogation	.09*	.02	.04	.19***	-.08*	-.44***	1.00		
8. Self-esteem	-.06	-.01	-.05	-.27***	.12***	.52***	-.61***	1.00	
9. Depressive affect	.10**	.06	.06*	.22***	-.14***	-.44***	.57***	-.44***	1.00
10. Mastery	-.10**	-.02	.00	-.27***	.14***	.46***	-.70***	.50***	-.55***
11. Peer support	-.01	.02	-.01	-.10**	-.02	.17***	-.11**	.10**	-.08*
12. Teacher support	-.04	-.03	-.06	-.21***	.12***	.22***	-.16***	.22***	-.13***
13. Time pressures at school	.01	-.01	.04	.00	-.07*	.09**	-.13***	.04	-.17***
14. Supervisor support	-.00	.08	.04	-.16**	.02	.18**	-.11*	.13*	-.10
15. Support from coworker	.08	.04	-.02	-.07	-.02	.04	.04	.02	.10
16. Work satisfaction	-.02	.07	.05	-.09	-.04	.25***	-.19***	.23***	-.14**
17. Low work stress	-.04	-.09	-.08	-.04	.20***	.07	-.05	.08	-.19***
18. Work is interesting	.00	.01	.02	-.10	.02	.13**	-.16**	.13**	-.17***

	10.	11.	12.	13.	14.	15.	16.	17.	18.
1. Father's employment status									
2. Change in family composition									
3. Geographical move									
4. Discomfort with parents									
5. Grade point average									
6. Well-being									
7. Self-derogation									
8. Self-esteem									
9. Depressive affect									
10. Mastery	1.00								
11. Peer support	.17***	1.00							
12. Teacher support	.23***	.17***	1.00						
13. Time pressures at school	.12***	.09**	.13***	1.00					
14. Supervisor support	.14*	.07	.17**	.06	1.00				
15. Support from coworker	-.01	.19**	.09	-.06	.19**	1.00			
16. Work satisfaction	.17***	.15**	.10*	.07	.29***	.04	1.00		
17. Low work stress	.12*	.19***	.17**	.16**	.20***	-.04	.13**	1.00	
18. Work is interesting	.12*	.02	.00	.13**	.32***	-.06	.43***	.22***	1.00

Note. N ranges from 708–956 for measures including the total panel, and from 288–449 for measures involving employed adolescents.
*$p < .05$. **$p < .01$. ***$p < .001$.

variables), and we are less interested in whether they continue to occur when covarying comforts (or stressors) in other arenas are controlled. There are significant correlations among the predictors (although all are quite small in magnitude).

However, it is necessary to include the direct effects of particular extrafamily comfort domains in the equations when estimating each one's moderative influence. That is, when testing whether supervisory support moderates the effects of parent–adolescent relationship discomfort on the adjustment outcomes, the direct effects of both supervisory support as well as family discomfort must be included in the equations.

FAMILY CHANGE AND DISCOMFORT
IN PARENT–ADOLESCENT RELATIONS

Because the objective change events (i.e., change in the father's employment status, change in family composition, or a geographical move) can influence the structure and daily routines of the family, it is plausible to assume that these changes could produce uncertainties and disruptions in adolescents' relationships with their parents, fostering discomfort in the parent–adolescent relationship (Path A). For example, Elder and colleagues (Elder et al., 1986) reported that fathers became more punitive and inconsistent under the strain of financial loss.

To assess the implications of family changes for the parent–adolescent relationship, discomfort with parents (a dichotomous construct) was regressed (using logistic regression) on each indicator of change (taken one at a time), the lagged outcome (discomfort with parents 1 year earlier), and background variables (parents' socioeconomic status [SES], race, nativity, and gender), all of which may affect the quality of the parent–child relationship (Baldwin et al., 1990; Barber & Thomas, 1986; LeCroy, 1989; Lempers et al., 1989; McLoyd, 1990; Nidorf, 1985; Steinberg, 1987).

Because this series of analyses indicates that the family changes do not significantly affect comfort in adolescents' relationships with parents, the findings are not shown. However, inclusion of family discomfort in the prior year as a predictor makes this analysis particularly stringent. For instance, the effects of divorce occur over a long period of time; the greatest difficulties may stem from the conflict and discord prior to the actual severance of the parental bond (Demo & Acock, 1988; Peterson & Zill, 1986). Thus, any effects of the divorce process could be registered in the lagged outcome variable and thus effectively controlled in the analysis. A similar argument could be made for other event stressors in the family (e.g., the father's job change or a geographical move). The impacts of prior stressors leading up to the actual event would be captured, at least in part, by the lagged family discomfort variable, diminishing the apparent effect of each change. Still the fact that there are no significant zero-order relationships between any of the acute events and family discomfort (see Table 5.1) reduces the credibility of the argument that the null findings are simply attributable to such overcontrol.

FAMILY CHANGE AND ADOLESCENT ADJUSTMENT

Although discomfort in the family (represented by an absence of supportive relations with either parent) seems rather impervious to the family changes, these events could still influence the adolescent's mental health and achievement. For example, the father's job loss or the family's movement to a new geographic area could produce feelings of insecurity and foreboding in an adolescent who already, because of an inherently ambiguous transitional status, feels ill at ease. Such circumstances would seemingly place adolescents at greater risk.

To examine this possibility, the adolescent outcomes were regressed on each change event in the family (change in the father's employment status, family composition, and geographical mobility) entered one at a time (Path E), controlling the same background indicators of advantage and disadvantage (included in earlier analyses) known to influence adolescent mental health and achievement (Baldwin et al., 1990; Clark, 1983; Furstenberg, 1988; McLoyd, 1990; Spencer et al., 1990), as well as the 1-year lagged outcome variables. (As already noted, in these analyses, direct effects of comfort in the extrafamilial arenas are not included.)

We do find that discrete family changes have deleterious consequences (data not shown in tabular form). Change in the father's employment status appears to foster negative psychological states in the adolescent: self-derogation (*beta* = .08, *p* < .05) and depressive affect (*beta* = .089, *p* < .05). However, change in the father's employment status is not related to the other mental health criteria (well-being, self-esteem, or perceived competence) or to academic performance. Change in family composition and a geographical move between the 9th and 10th grades both appear to reduce the level of academic achievement (*beta* = −.076, *p* < .01; *beta* = −.059, *p* < .05, respectively). However, change in family composition and moving had no significant impact on the mental health outcomes.

FAMILY DISCOMFORT AND ADOLESCENT
ADJUSTMENT

The effects of strained relationships with parents—that is, an absence of even one supportive parental relationship—on adolescents' mental health and academic achievement are represented by Path B of Fig. 5.1. It is possible that adolescents who suffer from depressed mood or those who have a poor self-image evaluate their relationships in the family arena less favorably than adolescents who manifest a higher level of well-being and self-esteem. They might also assess relationships and experiences in other domains less favorably. Controlling the ninth-grade mental health outcomes takes into account this potential source of spuriousness—the adolescent's stable proclivity to perceive relationships as comfortable or uncomfortable. Thus, when prior levels of psychological functioning are controlled, significant coefficients, reflecting the effects of discomfort, would provide support for the hypothesis that discomfort produces change in mental health over time. The same applies to the achievement outcome. Therefore, each of the criteria was regressed on family discomfort, again controlling the 1-year lagged mental health and achievement outcomes and the background variables.

Discomfort with parents is found to have a pervasive influence on the outcomes. An absence of comfort—with either parent—diminishes academic performance, psychological well-being, self-esteem, and mastery while heightening depressive affect and self-derogation (see Table 5.2).

Although not of central interest to us here, the effects of the background variables deserve comment. As the SES of the family increases, adolescents report higher GPAs and self-esteem. Consistent with much previous research (Allgood-Merten et al., 1990; Compas et al., 1998; Gecas, 1989; Maccoby & Jacklin, 1974; Petersen et al., 1991; Simmons & Blyth, 1987; Simmons, Burgeson, Carlton-Ford, & Blyth, 1987), girls' scores indicate poorer psychological functioning than boys on all five mental health scales: lower well-being, self-esteem, and mastery, and greater self-derogation and depressive affect. Whites manifest stronger tendencies toward self-derogation than minority adolescents.

EXTRAFAMILIAL COMFORT ARENAS, FAMILY
DISCOMFORT, AND ADOLESCENT ADJUSTMENT

Before examining extrafamilial arenas of comfort as conditioning factors, we ascertain whether each has direct effects influencing adolescents' perceptions of comfort with parents as well as the mental health and achievement outcomes. Having a larger support network might make the adolescent less dependent emotionally on family and thereby diffuse the potential for turbulent parent–child relations. Positive experiences at school and at work might also serve to alleviate tension in family relationships. To investigate such possibilities, family discomfort was regressed (using logistic regression) on each comfort indicator one at a time (in the

TABLE 5.2
Effects of Family Discomfort on 10th-Grade Adolescent Adjustment

Variable		Grade Point Average	Well-Being	Self-Derogation	Self-Esteem	Depressive Affect	Mastery
Family discomfort	β	-.137	-1.148	.342	-.880	1.465	-.683
	beta	-.080**	-.178***	.062*	-.163***	.123***	-.129***
Socioeconomic status	β	.042	-.015	-.023	.129	-.171	.001
	beta	.085**	-.008	-.015	.083**	-.050	.005
Race	β	.094	.082	.502	-.239	.145	-.385
(0 = minority, 1 = White)	beta	.049	.011	.080*	-.038	.010	-.063
Nativity	β	-.162	.047	-.426	.365	-.217	.279
(0 = foreign born, 1 = U.S. born)	beta	-.049	.004	-.039	.034	-.009	.027
Gender	β	-.001	.505	-.402	.475	-1.047	.346
(0 = girls, 1 = boys)	beta	-.005	.081*	-.076*	.091**	-.091**	.068*
Prior adjustment	β	.582	.335	.534	.472	.406	.472
(ninth grade)	beta	.580***	.319***	.506***	.439***	.395***	.443***
R^2		.408***	.159***	.302***	.271***	.208***	.263***
Number of cases		832	850	832	837	846	849

Note. *p < .05. **p < .01. ***p < .001.

105

peer, school, and work settings), family discomfort 1 year prior, and the background variables.

Supportive relationships with teachers (i.e., comfort at school) appear to lessen adolescents' discomfort with parents ($B = -.818, p < .001$), as does the absence of a sense of time pressure in the school setting ($B = -.369, p < .05$), even controlling prior family discomfort. None of the indicators of comfort in the peer and work domain, however, has direct effects on family discomfort.

To examine whether relationships and experiences outside the family influence adolescents' academic achievement and mental health, each of the outcomes was regressed on one measure of comfort (with friends, at school, or at work), again controlling the background variables and the 1-year lagged outcome variable. It should be noted that these analyses differ from the analyses reported in chapter 4, which also considered the effects of social support on adolescent development. First, as a preliminary step in our assessment of moderating conditions, the analyses presented here examine diverse sources of comfort, including interpersonal relationships as well as positive, gratifying nonpersonal experiences. Furthermore, whereas the analyses reported here examine each comfort indicator entered into the equations separately, the prior analyses examined cumulative support (proportion of comfortable domains among those available to the adolescent as indicated by the arenas of comfort index). Chapter 4 also examined the independent effects of each source of comfort in the various settings, net of the others, for both employed and nonemployed subgroups.

Having a peer (or peers) to turn to for support and understanding in times of trouble fosters adolescents' well-being, self-esteem, and sense of mastery, and diminishes both self-derogation and depressive affect (see Table 5.3). Having a comfortable friendship is found to have no significant effect, however, on academic performance.

Supportive and comfortable relationships at school were not associated with school achievement, but teacher support does have a significant impact on all variables reflecting adolescent mental health: increasing well-being, self-esteem, and competence, and decreasing self-derogation

TABLE 5.3
Effects of Peer Comfort on 10th-Grade Adolescent Adjustment
(Unstandardized Coefficients)

Comfort in Peer Group	Grade Point Average	Well-Being	Self-Derogation	Self-Esteem	Depressive Affect	Mastery
Peer support	—	.905***	-.662***	.562***	-1.076**	.797***

Note. All equations control socioeconomic status, race, nativity, gender, and prior adjustment. — indicates nonsignificant results.
*$p < .05$. **$p < .01$. ***$p < .001$.

and depressed mood (see Table 5.4). Whereas in chapter 4 we reported that comfort at school did not affect most mental health outcomes in either employed or nonemployed 10th-grade subgroups, as noted before, in the preceding analyses (see Tables 4.8 and 4.9) we controlled support in other domains of adolescents' lives. Thus, teacher support had but two statistically significant independent effects. In tandem, the findings would suggest that teacher support is not as critical for adolescents as support received from other sources, especially from family and peers. In addition, our analyses here, which extend to comforting experiences outside the interpersonal domain, show that being free of time pressures at school reduces adolescents' depressive affect.

The findings shown in Table 5.5 indicate direct benefits of comfort at work. These results may seem quite surprising given widespread concern about *youthwork* having a negative influence on adolescent development. To the contrary, job satisfaction fosters global feelings of well-being and lowers self-derogation and depressive affect. Reporting low levels of stress at work, also signifying comfort, enhances adolescents' well-being and self-esteem and reduces depressive affect. When work is perceived as interesting, depressive affect is likewise diminished. Moreover, experiencing support from a supervisor decreases employed adolescents' depressive affect and increases feelings of mastery. The presence of these significant consequences of supervisory support, and the absence of significant effects of comfort at work in the analyses presented in chapter 4 (see Table 4.9), are due both to differences in construct definition (comfort at work in chap. 4 only includes measures of relations with supervisor and friends at work) and model specification.

Of the various indicators of comfort in the work arena, support from a best friend at work is found to be the least consequential. Coworker support is not significantly related to adolescents' GPA or to any of the mental health outcomes.

It is surely noteworthy that peer support (Table 5.3) is found to have uniformly positive consequences for all the mental health indicators,

TABLE 5.4
Effects of School Comfort on 10th-Grade Adolescent Adjustment
(Unstandardized Coefficients)

Comfort in School	Grade Point Average	Well-Being	Self-Derogation	Self-Esteem	Depressive Affect	Mastery
Teacher support	—	.899***	−.529**	.555***	−1.166**	.856***
Low time pressures	—	—	—	—	−1.166**	—

Note. All equations control socioeconomic status, race, nativity, gender, and prior adjustment. — indicates nonsignificant results.
*p < .05. **p < .01. ***p < .001.

TABLE 5.5
Effects of Work Comfort on 10th-Grade Adolescent Adjustment
(Unstandardized Coefficients)

Comfort in School	Grade Point Average	Well-Being	Self-Derogation	Self-Esteem	Depressive Affect	Mastery
Supervisor support	—	—	—	—	-1.356*	.874**
Support from coworker	—	—	—	—	—	—
Work is satisfying	—	1.457***	-.718*	—	-1.735*	—
Low work stress	—	.852*	—	.906**	-2.410**	—
Work is interesting	—	—	—	—	-1.610**	—

Note. All equations control socioeconomic status, race, nativity, gender, and prior adjustment.

— indicates nonsignificant results.

*$p < .05$. **$p < .01$. ***$p < .001$.

whereas support from a best friend at work has no such effects (Table 5.5). This difference in the predictive power of the two variables, both reflecting relations with peers, may be attributable to the more superficial character of friendship within the work setting. Adolescents can voluntarily choose the friends they turn to in times of trouble from the wide range of acquaintances they have in all the various contexts in which they find themselves. In contrast, in the work setting, they are restricted to a smaller number of fellow employees who, given the transitory character of adolescent employment, may change frequently. Furthermore, Greenberger (1988) emphasized constraints to noninstrumental communications and to the formation of intimate relationships that are inherent in the modern workplace.

THE ARENA OF COMFORT AS MODERATOR

Earlier in this chapter, we reported that the three change events in the family are not direct sources of discomfort with parents. Nonetheless, it is plausible that their capacity to disrupt parent–adolescent relations would be contingent on the positive or negative character of the adolescent's experiences in extrafamily arenas. To investigate whether extrafamilial sources of comfort moderate the effects of family change on adolescents' perceptions of discomfort with parents (Path C of Fig. 5.1), family discomfort is regressed (using logistic regression) on the background variables, each measure of change included one at a time, one moderator (comfort in the peer, school, or work arenas), and the product of the same change and moderator variable. However, none of the interaction terms is significant.

Let us now turn to the foremost question at hand—the one that is most central to Simmons' (in press; Simmons & Blyth, 1987) formulation. Can supportive and positive experiences with friends at school or at work moderate the effects of family discomfort on adolescents' mental health and achievement (Path D of Fig. 5.1)? To examine the buffering effects of comfort, a series of analyses is performed. For example, taking the case of comfort with friends, each outcome is regressed on friend support, family discomfort, the product of family discomfort and friend support, the background variables, and the lagged outcome variable.

Again, because none of these interactions was found to be significant, we find no evidence that comfortable relationships with friends buffer the adverse effects of family discomfort on adolescent mental health and achievement. It should be noted, however, that the interaction terms that result from multiplying family discomfort with peer comfort is somewhat skewed because only a minority of adolescents (17.8%) is uncomfortable with both parents and comfortable with friends. Therefore, due to the small size of the referent group, it is possible that significant interactions are obscured. This same caution applies to the interaction of family discomfort with school and work comfort described next.

A similar series of analyses is performed with the measures of comfort at school. Indicators of comfort at school (teacher support and the lack of time pressures at school, considered one at a time), family discomfort, and the product of family discomfort and the same measure of comfort at school are included, along with the background and lagged variables. Again, none of the interaction terms reaches significance. Therefore, we conclude that supportive teacher–student relationships and a comfortable school experience do not moderate the effects of family discomfort on psychological adjustment.

Finally, we consider the workplace as a comfort arena, with analyses performed for all employed adolescents. Following the same procedure, each mental health and achievement outcome was regressed on one work moderator (supervisor support, support from a friend at work, job satisfaction, low levels of stress, and boredom at work, entered one at a time), family discomfort, the product of family discomfort and the same moderator, the background variables, and the lagged outcome. Significant coefficients for the product terms indicate that moderating effects are present; that is, family discomfort has different effects on the outcomes depending on the level of comfort at work.

Three interaction terms are found to be statistically significant (3 of 36, which is better than chance expectation): The interaction of family discomfort and support from a supervisor significantly influences well-being, self-esteem, and mastery. Because beta coefficients for interaction terms are not easily interpretable, regressions are performed separately for each condition (signifying the presence or absence of comfort) of the significant work moderators. For example, as shown in Table 5.6, Panel A, well-being in the 10th grade is regressed on 9th-grade well-being, discomfort with parents, and the background variables, separately for employed adolescents who have comfortable, supportive relationships with their supervisors and for those who do not.

Table 5.6 (Panels A–C) shows that family discomfort significantly influences adjustment only when employed adolescents do not have comfortable relationships with their supervisors at work. That is, when supervisor support is absent, family discomfort decreases employed adolescents' well-being, self-esteem, and mastery. Discomfort with parents is not significantly related to these outcomes when employed adolescents have positive relationships with their supervisors at work.

Can the presence of an arena of comfort buffer the effects of change in the family on mental health and academic performance (depicted by Path F of Fig. 5.1)? Following the same pattern, interaction analyses are again

TABLE 5.6
Moderating Effects of Work Comfort on the Relationship Between
Family Discomfort and 10th-Grade Adolescent Adjustment (Total Panel)

A. Well-Being	Supervisor Support Absent		Supervisor Support Present	
	β	beta	β	beta
Family discomfort	-1.384	-.221**	.195	.032
Socioeconomic status	-.149	-.072	.034	.020
Race	.256	.034	.797	.114
Nativity	1.136	.088	-.929	-.094
Gender	.926	.151*	-.295	-.052
Well-being (9th grade)	.370	.364***	.258	.280**
R^2		.251***		.093
Number of cases		199		105

B. Self-Esteem	Supervisor Support Absent		Supervisor Support Present	
	β	beta	β	beta
Family discomfort	-1.084	-.199**	.161	.031
Socioeconomic status	-.001	-.005	.032	.022
Race	-.116	-.018	-.870	-.146
Nativity	1.054	.100	1.311	.002
Gender	.266	.050	-.404	-.084
Self-esteem (9th grade)	.507	.444***	.517	.465***
R^2		.321***		.211**
Number of cases		199		105

C. Mastery	Supervisor Support Absent		Supervisor Support Present	
	β	beta	β	beta
Family discomfort	-1.145	-.212**	.403	.068
Socioeconomic status	.049	.027	.126	.080
Race	-.575	-.089	.397	.059
Nativity	.698	.068	-.568	-.059
Gender	.226	.042	.204	.038
Mastery (9th grade)	.513	.449***	.440	.401***
R^2		.279***		.170**
Number of cases		196		101

Note. *$p < .05$. **$p < .01$. ***$p < .001$.

111

performed (using OLS regression) to examine the moderating effects of comfort in extrafamily settings. (It should be noted that, using the available measures, few adolescents experienced family change. Therefore, the distribution of family change by peer comfort interaction terms are skewed, which may result in the suppression of significant interactions in the regression analyses. The same holds true for analyses described next, where family change is interacted with school and work comfort.)

Two significant interactions are revealed (2 of 18 interaction terms, or 11%): Comfort with friends moderates the consequences of change in father's employment status on adolescent self-esteem; comfort with friends also conditions the influence of a geographical move on perceived well-being. As shown in Table 5.7, Panel A, change in the father's employment status diminishes self-esteem when comfort with friends is present,

TABLE 5.7
Moderating Effects of Peer Comfort on the Relationship Between Family
Change and 10th-Grade Adolescent Adjustment (Total Panel)

	Peer Support Absent		Peer Support Present	
A. Self-Esteem	β	beta	β	beta
Change in father's employment status	.254	.021	−1.559	−.125**
Socioeconomic status	.014	.010	.022	.014
Race	−.795	−.127*	.044	.007
Nativity	.695	.068	−.189	−.018
Gender	1.129	.214***	.365	.070
Self-esteem (9th grade)	.417	.392***	.491	.463***
R^2	.266***		.250***	
Number of cases	257		389	

	Peer Support Absent		Peer Support Present	
B. Well-Being	β	beta	β	beta
Geographical change	1.012	.112*	−.381	−.044
Socioeconomic status	−.001	−.001	−.022	−.012
Race	−.096	−.013	.573	.078
Nativity	1.785	.150	−1.025	−.079
Gender	.890	.138**	.743	.117**
Well-being (9th grade)	.402	.400***	.277	.265***
R^2	.221***		.095***	
Number of cases	301		468	

Note. *p < .05. **p < .01. ***p < .001.

but this change in the family setting manifests no effect on self-esteem when comfort with friends is absent. However, this relationship is not in the predicted direction; that is, friend support does not ameliorate the presumed deleterious effects of change.

Turning to another counterintuitive pattern, in Panel B, a geographic move is associated with increased well-being when friend support is low, but has no significant impact on adolescent well-being when peer support is high. That is, a move at some point during the past year is associated with increased well-being for adolescents who report they have no close and supportive relationships with friends in the 10th grade. Again, this pattern is difficult to interpret. Possibly a move could be a welcome event for adolescents who do not have close and comfortable peer associations or if it meant escaping poor school and peer relations.

Do comfortable relationships and experiences at school (teacher support and an absence of time pressures at school) moderate the effects of family change on adolescent adjustment? Three interaction terms were found to be statistically significant (3 of 36, which is better than chance): Teacher support conditions the effect of a geographical move on academic performance; the indicator of time pressure conditions the effects of a geographical move on academic performance and depressive affect. Conditional analyses for the latter two interaction terms did not yield significant discomfort coefficients. Therefore, the results are not presented in tabular form.

Table 5.8 shows that moving has deleterious consequences for adolescent outcomes only when adolescents are not comfortable at school. That is, when teacher support is low, a geographical move is associated with a

TABLE 5.8

Moderating Effects of School Comfort on the Relationship Between
Family Change and 10th-Grade Adolescent Adjustment (Total Panel)

	Teacher Support Absent		Teacher Support Present	
A. Grade Point Average	β	beta	β	beta
Geographical move	−.280	−.124**	.007	.003
Socioeconomic status	.073	.144***	.024	.051
Race	.135	.067	.009	.005
Nativity	−.145	−.039	−.174	−.059
Gender	−.009	−.005	−.007	−.004
Grade point average (9th grade)	.597	.600***	.554	.552***
R^2		.489***		.341***
Number of cases		369		466

Note. *$p < .05$. **$p < .01$. ***$p < .001$.

drop in the student's GPA. When teacher support is high, moving does not significantly affect academic performance.

Do relationships and experiences at work (supervisor support, support from a friend at work, satisfaction, low levels of stress, and boredom at work) moderate the effects of family change on academic performance and mental health? Eight interaction terms are found to be significant (8 of 90, or 8.9%, which is slightly better than chance). Specifically, the adolescent's own work stress conditions the effects of change in the father's employment status on self-esteem. Work stress also conditions the effect of a geographical move on self-derogation. The impact of change in family composition on well-being is found to be contingent on support from a best friend at work. In addition, support from a friend at work moderates the effect of moving on adolescent mastery. Work satisfaction conditions the effect of moving on self-esteem. Finally, having interesting work moderates the effects of moving on well-being, self-esteem, and mastery.

The results of four conditional analyses, all involving the effects of moving for those who find comfort or an absence of comfort at work, were not significant and therefore are not presented. However, as shown in Table 5.9, Panel A, change in the father's employment status diminishes self-esteem only when work stress is high. When work stress is low (indicating a comfortable state), change in the father's employment status has no significant effect on employed adolescents' self-esteem.

Change in family composition decreases well-being for employed adolescents who are not comfortable with a friend at work. In contrast, a change in family composition is associated with increased well-being for workers who have a supportive work friend. Panel C shows that a geo-

TABLE 5.9

Moderating Effects of Work Comfort on the Relationship Between
Family Change and 10th-Grade Adolescent Adjustment (Total Panel)

	High Work Stress		Low Work Stress	
A. Self-Esteem	β	beta	β	beta
Change in father's employment status	−5.932	−.493**	−.682	−.054
Socioeconomic status	.074	.047	.022	.013
Race	.906	.165	−1.059	−.148**
Nativity	−.670	−.067	1.563	.144*
Gender	.391	.075	.283	.054
Self-esteem (9th grade)	.596	.461**	.432	.393***
R^2	.381***		.207***	
Number of cases	44		309	

(Continued)

TABLE 5.9
(Continued)

B. Well-Being	Coworker Support Absent β	beta	Coworker Support Present β	beta
Change in family composition	−1.745	−.190*	1.628	.192*
Socioeconomic status	−.077	−.041	.019	.010
Race	.129	.017	.292	.039
Nativity	.310	.024	−.861	−.072
Gender	.698	.116	.701	.122
Well-being (9th grade)	.280	.245**	.341	.401***
R^2	.113***		.235***	
Number of cases	172		137	

C. Mastery	Coworker Support Absent β	beta	Coworker Support Present β	beta
Geographical move	1.219	.165*	−.596	−.075
Socioeconomic status	.153	.097	.064	.039
Race	−.469	−.072	.599	.092
Nativity	.969	.095	.011	.001
Gender	.278	.055	.030	.006
Mastery (9th grade)	.521	.456***	.461	.402***
R^2	.266***		.166***	
Number of cases	171		133	

D. Mastery	Work Is Boring β	Beta	Work Is Interesting β	beta
Geographical move	−.671	−.090	.966	.124*
Socioeconomic status	.167	.098	.019	.012
Race	−.497	−.071	.163	.025
Nativity	1.249	.119	.079	.007
Gender	.510	.097	.076	.015
Mastery (9th grade)	.475	.415***	.511	.478***
R^2	.218***		.244***	
Number of cases	120		286	

Note. *$p < .05$. **$p < .01$. ***$p < .001$.

115

graphic move increases perceptions of mastery when workers do not have a comfortable relationship with a coworker; this result is difficult to explain. When support from a coworker is high, moving has no significant impact on competence. Table 5.9, Panel D demonstrates that moving has no impact on mastery when work is boring; however, when work is described as interesting, moving increases adolescents' sense of mastery. Thus, relationships and experiences at work appear to buffer the effects of change on employed adolescents' mental health.

SUMMARY AND DISCUSSION

The concept of an arena of comfort draws attention to the multiplicity of social contexts in which human development occurs and the degree of congruence of experiences among these various domains. The ecology of the life space becomes a central concern of developmental psychology (Bronfenbrenner, 1986) and the study of stress (Eckenrode & Gore, 1990; Thoits, 1995) as the adolescent's social world expands (Jackson & Rodriguez-Tome, 1993). The research presented in this chapter contributes to our knowledge of cross-domain buffering effects; the interrelations of family, friends, school, and work during adolescence; and their implications for adolescents' mental health and achievement.

We report evidence that some experiences of objective change in the family, as well as discomfort in relationships with parents, may have adverse consequences for adolescents. However, supporting the contention that chronic stressors are more predictive of mental health than major life events (Delongis et al., 1982; Rowlinson & Felner, 1988), ongoing strain (i.e., discomfort with parents) is found to have more negative consequences for adolescent adjustment than did the life event stressors such as changes in family composition. Specifically, strained or uncomfortable relationships with parents diminish adolescents' sense of well-being, self-esteem, and self-efficacy, and heighten depressive affect. Discomfort with parents is also linked to a lower level of school achievement. The family changes under consideration have more delimited consequences. Change in the father's employment status is found to be associated with diminished mental health—that is, an increase in negative self-concept or self-derogation and depressive affect. Adolescents who experience change in their families—changes linked to shifts in the composition of the household and a geographic move—do not do as well in school as those who do not experience such changes during the previous year.

Somewhat surprisingly, the change events were found to have no significant impact on adolescents' relationships with their parents. Neither were the arenas of comfort found to modify the effects of change in the family on discomfort with parents. Perhaps the circumstances preceding these events, occurring prior to the initiation of the Youth Development Study, would have more profound impacts on perceptions of comfort with parents. However, such deleterious consequences, if they do occur, may be rather transient.

Extrafamilial sources of social support and comfort are shown to enhance parent–adolescent relationships. That is, having supportive relationships with teachers is found to diminish perceptions of discomfort with parents. At this time of disengagement from parents and increasing autonomy, being able to establish one or more positive relationships with teachers or other respected adults outside the family may signify to the parent (and to the adolescent) movement toward a more mature, interpersonally skilled social being. Moreover, experiencing the school setting as comfortable, as indicated by a lack of time pressures, also appears to lessen the likelihood of family discomfort.

Positive relationships with friends and teachers are clearly associated with enhanced mental health (e.g., increasing adolescents' well-being, self-esteem, and mastery, and decreasing self-derogation and depressed mood). Employed adolescents' support from their supervisors goes along with diminished depressive affect and stronger competence. Thus, support from people outside the family—from friends, teachers, and work supervisors—appears to be related to positive adolescent development.

Furthermore, comfortable experiences at work are found to enhance the mental health indicators. When young people report that their work is interesting, they also indicate less depressive affect. Having low levels of stress at work is associated with heightened well-being and self-esteem, and less depressed mood. Young people who are more satisfied with their jobs report higher levels of global well-being and manifest less self-derogation and depressive affect. Thus, contrary to a popular stereotype that youthwork is quite uniform in character, consisting of low-level, repetitive jobs that do not evoke a sense of challenge or interest, we find evidence that complexity and variety in adolescent work has positive developmental consequences. The fact that a wide range of indicators of social advantage and disadvantage are controlled, along with lagged outcome variables, provides confidence that these findings are not spurious.

From the standpoint of Simmons' (in press; Simmons & Blyth, 1987) arena of comfort model, however, these are not the most critical findings of this research. Most significant from this cross-context perspective are the wide-ranging conditional influences revealed by our analysis. Can comfort in one sphere—in this case, in a domain outside the family—buffer the negative developmental consequences of strain and discomfort within the family? To gauge the effects of family strain, we identify a situation in the family that, on the face of it, clearly lacks comfort—when the adolescent does not report a positive, supportive relationship with either parent—with a more positive family environment—when the adolescent has a supportive relationship with at least one parent. Much evidence points to an affirmative answer to this key question: Comfort that adolescents draw on from outside the family can buffer the detrimental effects of strained relationships with parents.

Our analysis compares the adjustment of adolescents who have supportive or strained relations with parents under conditions of greater or lesser comfort elsewhere. It is particularly noteworthy that it is comfort in the workplace, not with friends or at school, that effectively buffers the deleterious influence of family discomfort on adolescent adjustment. The quality of parent–child relationships is found to have quite different implications for youth mental health depending on whether social support is available in the work setting. Strained relationships with both parents diminish employed adolescents' well-being, self-esteem, and mastery only when relationships with work supervisors are also uncomfortable. However, when the adolescent has established a supportive relationship with a supervisor, the absence of a good relationship with a parent no longer appears to matter for these important outcomes. Apparently adolescents who are able to seek out and establish relationships with supervisors at work thereby protect themselves when there is discord in the family. The very act of establishing a supportive relationship in this domain may provide, to the self and others, evidence of positive movement toward a more mature status. Thereby the adolescent constructs the context in which further development occurs.

We find further conditional effects in our analyses of the consequences of three discrete or eventlike changes in the family: geographic mobility, shifts in household composition, and a change in the father's employment status. Here again, stressors presumably associated with change do not have negative developmental consequences when comfort is found outside the family setting. In the arena of the school, supportive relationships with teachers buffer the negative consequences of a geographical move for adolescent achievement. When adolescents perceive little support from teachers, moving appears to reduce academic achievement. However, moving has no demonstrable effect on achievement under more comfortable circumstances at school.

Moreover, for those adolescents who are employed, comfortable relationships and experiences in the work setting are found to buffer the effects of family change on mental health. That is, change in the father's employment status has no manifest influence on self-esteem under conditions of low work stress. However, when work stress is high, this change diminishes employed adolescents' self-esteem. Change in family composition reduces well-being when adolescents do not have a comfortable relationship with a friend at work. In contrast, when support from a friend at work is available, change in family composition enhances well-being. Moving boosts adolescents' feelings of competence when work is considered interesting, but has no influence on mastery when work is described as boring.

Admittedly, not all tested interactions were statistically significant nor were all those that were revealed by the analysis in the expected direction. For example, in the absence of comfort with a friend, moving appears to enhance adolescent well-being. For adolescents who do not have comfortable peer relations, moving could represent an escape from an intolerable situation. Moreover, when the adolescent reports comfortable, supportive relationships with friends, change in the father's employment status appears to reduce self-esteem. It could be that the adolescent whose sense of self is most threatened seeks out comfort from friends, reversing the presumed causal ordering in our model. However, these interpretations of two anomalous patterns are post hoc and therefore suspect. Clearly, exploration of the conditions under which arenas of comfort ameliorate and exacerbate strain is in order.

The arena of comfort model specifies that sources of comfort within a given setting will be less effective buffers of stressors within that setting than comfort outside of it. Contrary to Simmons' (in press) thesis, the stressors we examine in this study—change in the family and discomfort in relations with parents—might possibly be buffered by relationships and experiences within the very same setting (e.g., by supportive relations with siblings, grandparents, or other relatives who reside in the home, or by satisfying recreational or productive activities within that setting). Unfortunately, the data at hand do not permit such further assessment of the arenas of comfort hypothesis. What the analyses do show is that comfort outside a major stressor context for adolescents, that of the family, has demonstrable buffering effects.

In conclusion, we offered some evidence that the experience of comfort outside the family reduces the negative consequences of change and strain within it. Having positive, comfortable experiences at work and at school helps adolescents cope with both change and discomfort in the family setting. Moreover, it is not only social support that has this buffering effect. In school and work settings, essentially productive, achievement-oriented settings, satisfying and engaging instrumental activities may be especially beneficial, offering distraction from the interpersonal strains and tensions at home as well as opportunities to demonstrate mastery and thereby enhance both coping skills and the self-concept. The presence of a comfort arena, through its provision of social support as well as gratifying and growth-inducing experiences, may strengthen the individual so that challenges in other life spheres can be dealt with effectively.

CHAPTER SIX

Arenas of Comfort
in Adolescence

An arena of comfort, as formulated by Simmons and colleagues (Simmons & Blyth, 1987; Simmons, Burgeson, Carlton-Ford, & Blyth, 1987), is a social context in which individuals can relax, feel at ease with themselves, and let down their guard. A comfort arena provides a safe and accepting place for the person to relax and rejuvenate so that stressors in other locations of the life space can be endured or overcome. This study addressed key questions surrounding the comfort construct. In this chapter, we summarize what we learned through this empirical assessment—the contribution this research makes to an understanding of adolescent development and ameliorative intervention. Finally, we suggest fruitful directions for further investigation.

THE QUALITY OF ADOLESCENT EXPERIENCE

At the heart of this study is a most basic, fundamental insight: The quality of experience matters. Although this point may seem obvious, it is sometimes lost in the altogether reasonable attempt to simplify and quantify environmental influences. Analysts focus on exposure to particular activities or domains, or to the temporal dimension of experience, rather than to its substantive content, phenomenal meaning, or affective quality. For example, given the importance of schooling in the status attainment process, there is great interest in educational achievement, gauged by the number of years young people spend in school or by the degrees or other credentials they receive as a result. Analysts measure the amount of time adolescents spend in various activities—hours spent doing homework, time spent with family and friends, and involvement in various extracurricular activities. As a case in point, the study of adolescent work experience is almost exclusively concerned with the intensity of that experience as indicated by the number of hours teenagers spend on the job each week.

To point out that the quality of experience matters in these various domains of family, peer group, school, and workplace may appear to be so obvious as to go unmentioned. However, explicitly acknowledging this truism opens up a Pandora's box of difficult, thorny issues: What are the key dimensions of experience in a given setting that would make a difference for adolescent mental health and achievement? Should the focus be on objective features of experiences or subjective reactions to them? By what criteria can the importance of a given type of experience be judged? Once pertinent experiences are identified, how can they be measured? Questions such as these have been the subject of a great deal of controversy and debate, extending well beyond the scope of this particular study (see Kohn et al., 1983).

Simmons' (in press) attempt to address these critical questions starts from the premise that the many developmental demands placed on adolescents make this stage of life inherently stressful. The adolescent must adapt to dramatic changes in bodily shape and other biological changes accompanying puberty, growing independence in relations with parents, new intimacy in peer relations, increasing impersonality and achievement pressures in the school setting, and many other changes. Given these diverse challenges, what becomes most important according to Simmons' (in press) analysis is having a context or role-relationship that "provides a warm, nonjudgmental social environment, where acceptance is unconditional. Here is where one feels 'at home', where one feels at peace with oneself, where one can 'let one's hair down' " (p. 22).

Thus, Simmons (in press) emphasized the adolescent's subjective reaction within a context as the key feature of experience: feelings of *comfort*—familiarity, calmness, satisfaction, and ease—and the availability of supportive relationships that nurture and sustain positive self-concepts. For Simmons, comfort is a subjective reaction and becomes a means of characterizing domains of involvement. The operationalizations of comfort used in this research were intended to capture this feature of adolescents' experience in the family, with peers, in school, and in work settings. Only adolescents who described their relationships and experiences in quite positive terms were considered to be comfortable.

Simmons' (in press) conceptualization of comfort points to the importance of support from others who affirm the person's self-image and provide complete acceptance—virtues, faults, and all. For an arena to have the capacity to moderate stressors in other contexts, the predictability of acceptance and support from other people is essential. Considering social support as the key indicator of comfort enabled us to establish consistency in the measurement of comfort across four major settings of adolescent involvement. This simplified a substantial part of the analysis (presented in chaps. 3 and 4) both conceptually and empirically.

However, feelings of comfort are not only derived from other people who provide support and affirmation. Bandura (1986, 1997) and Rutter (1990) drew attention to the developmental significance of experiences of success. By becoming engaged in an activity and working unself-consciously toward a goal, adolescents learn about themselves and their capabilities (Csikszentmihalyi & Larson, 1984). Such *flow* experiences are gratifying or comforting in themselves. Our noninterpersonal indicators of comfort in the school and work setting—referencing satisfaction, engagement, and the absence of stress—are thereby justified.

In recent years, developmentalists have become increasingly aware that assessment of the ecology of adolescent life, including multiple contexts and the interrelations among them, is necessary for an understanding of adolescent development (Cairns, Cairns, Rodkin, & Xie, 1998; Caspi & Moffitt, 1995; Steinberg & Avenevoli, 1998). However, empirical research on adolescence still typically focuses on one or just two contexts of development, often considered apart from other domains. In contrast, we examine perceptions of supportive and comfortable experiences in four arenas. In chapter 3, we ask: How is the phenomenal experience of comfort distributed in the adolescent life space? Do adolescents typically find comfort in just one or two or in all the identified spheres? Where are they most likely to experience this positive, comfortable state?

Chapter 3 describes adolescents' experience of comfort in the family, school, peer, and work arenas over a 3-year period extending from freshman to junior year of high school. When each of the contexts is examined singly, it becomes apparent that each is a highly prevalent source of comfort. For example, a majority of the young people find comfort in the family. Although adolescent–parent conflict is emphasized in popular renditions of Sturm und Drang (Maggs, Schulenberg, & Hurrelmann, 1997), we find that most adolescents (nearly 60%) report comfortable relationships with their mothers in all 3 years of this study. Clearly, mothers are strong sources of support.

One might think that egalitarian trends in the family, moving away from the traditional authoritarian, disciplining father counteracted by the warm and nurturant mother, would enhance comfort for contemporary adolescents in their relations with fathers. However, only a minority of adolescents (e.g., about a third of 10th graders) in this study report that their relations with their fathers are comfortable. Apparently discomfort and a degree of tension in father–child relations is typical of adolescent life.

It is often noted that adolescence is a period in which peer friendships assume great importance (Brown et al., 1997; Csikszentmihalyi & Larson, 1984; Savin-Williams & Berndt, 1990). Our findings provide confirmation: The proportion of adolescents who report comfortable relationships with friends is high and appears to increase over the years of observation. The prevalence of comfort with peers is, in fact, quite similar to that experienced with mothers.

Although there are certainly structural constraints to establishing close relationships with teachers during high school (i.e., large class size, movement among different classes each day), the majority of adolescents also indicate comfortable, supportive relations with their teachers. As can be gauged by their report of time pressures at school, most adolescents seem to feel comfortable with coursework obligations.

Similarly, the vast majority of adolescents who are employed find their work experiences to be satisfying, low in stress, and interesting (Mortimer et al., 1992a, 1992b; Mortimer, Finch, Dennehy, Lee, & Beebe, 1994). However, most young people do not appear to find very much social support in the work setting. Many employed adolescents do not have supervisors who could act as sources of support; given the high employee turnover typical of the jobs they hold, establishing close friendships at work may be difficult. Of those adolescents who have paid jobs, more than a third report feeling comfortable with supervisors (if they have them) and with friends at work.

Although these aggregate trends are interesting, Simmons' (in press) perspective directs attention to a more person-centered analysis focused on each individual's configuration of comfort. That is, it is not sufficient to know that the majority of adolescents find comfort in each setting; the same persons who do not have this presumably beneficial emotional state in one sphere may also not experience it in the others. The concept of an arena of comfort (Simmons & Blyth, 1987) acknowledges that individuals have multiple identities, that they enact a number of role-relationships, and that they participate in several contexts daily. Following the work of Linville (1985) and Thoits (1983), Simmons and Blyth (1987) hypothesized that persons experience better mental health and use more effective coping strategies if they are involved in multiple independent roles and if at least one context, or set of role-relationships, remains generally positive and stable.

Almost the entirety of the panel (approximately 90%) were found to be comfortable in at least one domain, and the majority of the adolescents (more than 60%) manifested feelings of comfort in two or more contexts. Thus, if one considers the absence of comfort to indicate a high degree of risk, only about 10% of the adolescents in the Youth Development Study would so qualify, and even these youth may have other sources of social support and satisfying activities in their lives that we have not measured. Furthermore, experiences of comfort were found to become more prevalent as adolescents mature: The proportion of arenas deemed comfortable (among those in which they participate) increased between the 9th and 11th grades for both girls and boys.

THE SOCIAL LOCATION OF COMFORT

These trends are surely reassuring because they suggest that comfortable social relationships and/or other gratifying experiences are widely obtained by adolescents in a variety of settings. Relatively few adolescents lack comfort in any of the four contexts to which we attend. However, we must take into account differences in comfort across societal categories. According to Simmons (in press), broad societal forces influence the capacity to find comfort. This assertion implies that the availability of comfort varies by the person's structural location. We investigated differences in experiences of comfort depending on gender, race, nativity, socioeconomic status (SES), and family composition. The analyses point to two relative deficiencies in comfort: among boys, who are less likely to experience comfort across a variety of settings than girls; and among adolescents in single-parent (and other nontraditional) family arrangements.

Of the various subgroup comparisons, gender emerged as the key discriminator. For example, although adolescents in the Youth Development Study, as in prior studies (Barber & Thomas, 1986; LeCroy, 1989; Steinberg, 1987), are much more likely to report comfort in relationships with their mothers than with their fathers, same-gender pairs are apparently more comfortable. Girls are more likely to report comfortable relations with their mothers than are boys, and boys are more comfortable with their fathers than are the girls.

In general, however, with respect to the experience of comfort, girls have the advantage. Girls are more likely than boys to report peer support—that they have a friend to turn to in times of trouble. Furthermore, girls who are employed perceive their work to be less stressful than boys (see also Mortimer et al., 1992a, 1992b). Girls who have jobs are also more comfortable with their friends at work than employed boys.

Adolescents from two-parent homes were more likely to find comfort in relationships with both their mothers and their fathers, and to have more comfortable experiences at work (as indicated by descriptions of how stressful or interesting their jobs are), than adolescents in single-parent families and those in other living arrangements.

In addition to examining single sources of comfort in relation to social location, we assessed differences in cumulative support as measured by the comfort index. This index, to some degree, reflects social inequality. Although we do not find differences between minority and White adolescents (consistent with Simmons, 1978) or between those who are foreign and native born, adolescents from higher socioeconomic backgrounds find support across a larger proportion of arenas. Consistent with our single-domain analyses, girls appear to be comfortable in a greater proportion of arenas than boys throughout the 3-year period. This pattern supports widespread beliefs that girls are more social or interpersonally oriented and perhaps also more socially skilled than boys (Gilligan, 1982).

THE ECOLOGY OF COMFORT, ADOLESCENT MENTAL HEALTH, AND ACHIEVEMENT

A large body of evidence demonstrates that perceived social support promotes coping and adjustment (Cohen & Wills, 1985; House et al., 1988; Kessler & McLeod, 1985; Masten & Coatsworth, 1995; Robinson & Garber, 1995; Savin-Williams & Berndt, 1990). Much research (reviewed in prior chapters) has confirmed the developmental benefits to be derived from supportive relationships, experiences of success, and gratifying experiences in each of the single domains under consideration: the family, peer group, the school, and the workplace. A key contribution of our study is to show the cumulative impacts of comfort across the life-space ecology.

As Simmons and her colleagues proposed (Simmons, in press; Simmons & Blyth, 1987; Simmons et al., 1987), having multiple sources of comfort is found to be consequential for adolescents' mental health. As the number of comfort arenas increases, positive psychological adjustment is enhanced, thereby improving adolescents' coping capacities and chances for future success. Chapter 4 documents clear benefits for adolescents with multiple sources of comfort. In general, adolescents who report more arenas in which they are provided with social support (considered as a proportion of those that are available to them) manifest a stronger sense of well-being, a more positive self-concept (reflected in indexes of self-derogation, self-esteem, and mastery), and lower levels of depressed mood. This is true even when the influence of background variables (race, nativity, SES, and family composition) and the mental health dimensions 1 year prior are taken into account.

Following the work of Stryker (1980) and Thoits (1983), Simmons and Blyth (1987) asserted that some interpersonal contexts will be more important than others to the person's self-image (see also Lepore, 1992). When we examine the independent, additive effects of the comfort arenas, comfortable relationships with parents appear to be more consequential to adolescents' mental health than supportive relationships with friends, teachers, supervisors, and/or a best friend at work. This is not to say that other sources of social support are unimportant, only that their influence appears to be less pervasive. The continuing significance of relations with parents for adolescent mental health, despite the adolescent's growing autonomy, is quite consistent with prior research (Galambos & Ehrenberg, 1997; Gecas & Seff, 1991; Jessor & Jessor, 1977; LeCroy, 1989; Maccoby & Martin, 1983; Mortimer, Lorence, & Kumka, 1986; Steinberg & Silverberg, 1986).

As might be expected given their acquisition of an adultlike social role, we find that working adolescents' mental health is somewhat less responsive to the quality of parent–adolescent relationships than that of their nonemployed counterparts. It could be that teenagers' entry into the adultlike world of work promotes a degree of disengagement from the family that reduces their vulnerability to discomfort within it.

Gender differences in reactions to comfort were also apparent. Congruent with prior studies (Douvan & Adelson, 1966; Gilligan, 1982; Richards & Larson, 1989), we find evidence that girls are more responsive and vulnerable to the quality of their social relationships than boys. This evidence—that the ecology of comfort across key dimensions of adolescent life has significant impacts on mental health—is wholly consistent with Simmons' (in press; Simmons & Blyth, 1987) formulation.

THE ARENA OF COMFORT'S MODERATING POWER

The central interest of Simmons (in press; Simmons & Blyth, 1987) draws us to the consideration of moderating effects. This concern is likewise integrally tied to the ecology of the life space. They posited that having an arena of comfort buffers the negative effects of change and discomfort, providing a place for the adolescent to step back and recover from stressors in other contexts. Thus, it is not possible to fully understand the consequences of experiences in particular arenas of involvement without knowledge of what is going on in other domains of the adolescent's life. Their insight implies the essential futility of attempting to explain or predict the course of adolescent development while only scrutinizing single domains of action. Hence, valid developmental investigations must encompass multiple dimensions of the life space.

The very concept of a comfort arena implies context-specific experiential resources that strengthen the person's ability to cope with change and discomfort in other domains. The attention to cross-domain buffering processes extends the conceptualization of stress and moderating processes. As suggested by Simmons and Blyth (1987), the more segregated role-relationships are, the more likely one arena can buffer disruption and discomfort experienced in another.

Considering the contextual features of the stress process, Simmons and Blyth (1987; Simmons et al., 1987) pointed out that disruption across many spheres of life can be overwhelming. They argued that it is not simply the accumulation of risk that is harmful. Rather, change occurring at the same time in numerous contexts is more detrimental to well-being than several changes occurring in one or two isolated arenas. Given the scope of the available data, this particular hypothesis—concerning changes in multiple versus single arenas—could not be empirically addressed. Instead, we consider whether comfort in the peer, school, or work settings moderates the effects of change, as well as discomfort, in one crucially important setting—that of the family.

Consistent with much other research, we find that changes experienced within the family arena as well as ongoing, chronic strain in the family context have adverse consequences for adolescents' mental health and academic performance (Compas, Davis, Forsythe, & Wagner, 1986; Rowlinson & Felner, 1988). However, it appears from the analysis that strained parent–adolescent relations are more detrimental than the family change events (i.e., change in father's employment and family composition or geographic moves). Because the experience of a supportive parent–adolescent relationship is so consequential for adolescent adjustment, it is especially important to understand how those who lack this resource can cope.

Comfort from outside the family (the stressor context in this analysis) is found to be protective in several ways. First, supportive relationships with teachers and low time pressure at school diminish adolescents' perceptions of discomfort with parents. In addition, as shown by the analyses presented in chapters 4 and 5, comfortable relationships and experiences in the peer, school, and work arenas increase well-being, self-esteem, and mastery, and decrease self-derogation and depressive affect.

With respect to the buffering effects, support from supervisors at work is found to moderate the effect of family discomfort on employed adolescents' well-being, self-esteem, and mastery. The special capacity of supervisor support to protect adolescents in the face of negative familial experience is particularly interesting. Work comfort (i.e., low work stress and support from a best friend at work) also was found to moderate the effects of family change stressors (i.e., change in father's employment status and family composition) on self-esteem and well-being. In view of the real dangers of overwork and exploitation in the workplace (Committee on the Health and Safety Implications of Child Labor, 1998), the potential of the work environment to exert a positive influence on adolescents' lives is often overlooked. Apparently finding comfort in the adultlike domain of work enables some adolescents to be relatively impervious to changes, tensions, and stressors in the family setting.

Although comfort in the peer and school settings did not diminish the negative consequences of strained relationships with parents, they did have other buffering effects. Comfortable school relationships (i.e., teacher support) and experiences (i.e., the absence of stress at school) were found to moderate the impacts of family change (e.g., a geographical move) on adolescent academic performance and depressed mood.

In summary, it appears that comfortable relationships and experiences in the peer, school, and work arenas help adolescents cope with stressors at home in several ways. These extrafamilial sources of comfort operate through their direct effects on perceptions of discomfort in the parent–adolescent relationship and on adolescents' psychological adjustment. Particularly germane to Simmons' (in press; Simmons & Blyth, 1987) hypothesis, they also have conditional effects in buffering the harmful consequences of change and discomfort in the family setting.

POTENTIAL FOR ADOLESCENT AGENCY

Simmons and colleagues (Simmons, in press; Simmons & Blyth, 1987; Simmons et al., 1987) emphasized the importance of balancing experiences of challenge and comfort as adolescents move between various settings. Whereas encountering and mastering challenging situations is essential for psychological growth (Shanahan & Mortimer, 1996), the process of developing coping skills, and thereby the increased capacity to deal with future challenges in life, is often stressful. Exposure to problematic situations early on in a sense inoculates the adolescent against adverse consequences in similar situations (Rutter, 1990). However, Simmons and Blyth's (1987) analysis implies that a degree of comfort, preferably obtained in settings that are external to the stressor, is necessary if such early coping efforts are to result in effective *steeling*. Acquiring the capacity to handle life's stresses and adversities, which derive both from interpersonal difficulties and complex, problematic tasks, thus requires rejuvenating social support and experiential satisfactions.

These considerations draw attention to the active role of the individual in coping and development (Caspi & Moffitt, 1995; Lerner, 1985; Robinson & Garber, 1995; Rutter, 1990). Environmental influences are, by their very nature, external to the person. However, they are not independent of the person's influence. In actuality, the person and environment are truly reciprocal in their effects on one another. Thus, some adolescents may have special capacities to draw sympathy, liking, and support from their peers and adults, who then can be drawn on for support in times of trouble. Individuals make choices based on their intentions and goals, both short and long term (Brandtstaedter, 1998). Simmons (in press) and others (Gecas, 1986; Gecas & Seff, 1990) noted that, although persons cannot exercise choice over all of the arenas in which they are involved, when allowed to choose they will gravitate toward contexts that protect their feelings of comfort with self. The selection of environments that promote comfort and the cultivation of relationships that offer social support are crucial dynamic processes.

For optimum development, however, the adolescent must not only seek out those contexts and role-relationships that offer support, acceptance, satisfaction, and security, but also those that, although discomforting in the short run, offer opportunities for challenge and long-term growth. Students of development must be as attuned to opportunities for growth in problematic situations (Galambos & Ehrenberg, 1997) as they have been to accompanying stressors and strains.

The significance of gender in our analyses becomes especially interesting in this regard. It appears that girls are more effective in selecting, finding, or constructing comforting environments. Girls are found to be more comfortable than boys with their mothers, friends, and best friends at work, and they perceive support across a larger proportion of their arenas of involvement. Interpersonal relationships may be more salient to girls (Gilligan, 1982; Richards & Larson, 1989), and this salience could be reflected in their more favorable appraisals. Girls may also be more skilled in developing supportive relationships.

Although comfort appears to moderate the detrimental effects of family change and poor relations with parents at least as well for girls as for boys, the fact that girls are more likely to find comfort in nonfamily settings appears to provide them with a distinct advantage. Girls as well as boys who are comfortable across a greater proportion of arenas experience better psychological adjustment. Then why are girls found to have lower scores on indicators of mental health? Numerous studies testify to girls' poorer self-images and elevated depressed mood during adolescence (Allgood-Merten et al., 1990; Compas et al., 1998; Gecas, 1989; Maccoby & Jacklin, 1974; Petersen et al., 1991; Simmons et al., 1979; Simmons et al., 1973).

This seeming paradox gives rise to several plausible interpretations. Evaluating their merit would carry us well beyond the scope of this particular study, but considering this somewhat perplexing constellation of findings could point to fruitful directions for future inquiry. Are we simply confronted with a social desirability bias—that is, girls' greater proclivity to present themselves and their relationships in a positive light? Alternatively, if the adolescent (and child in an earlier phase) is indeed an active agent in constructing the social scaffold of supports and comforts, it could be that distress increases the salience of and engagement in this very process. That is, girls may be especially oriented toward seeking out others and developing comfortable arenas, given their greater felt need for comfort, deriving from all the various stressors in early adolescence that Simmons and Blyth (1987) so well described. Comfort arenas may be intentionally constructed as a means of coping with life's adversities or perceived deficiencies within the self. Much additional study is necessary to understand the processes through which the child's and adolescent's active exercise of agency results in different amounts and constellations of comfort across settings.

IMPLICATIONS FOR INTERVENTION AND RESEARCH

Many adolescents suffer from poor self-concepts, a sense of inefficacy, depressive affect, and school difficulties. Do the findings of this study have any bearing on programs to prevent or ameliorate such problems? Most generally, the research indicates that a focus on contexts is worthwhile. Although interventions are often focused on changing adolescents, as when therapy, counseling, or special classes are offered, this research indicates that making adolescents' contexts more supportive and comfortable will be reflected in improved mental health and achievement. Effective interventions could be targeted toward enhancing adolescents' acceptance and affirmation by others and toward providing young people with tasks that yield a sense of accomplishment and success. Consistent with Lerner's *developmental contextualism*, interventions can focus on "the developmental system in which people are embedded" (Lerner, Ostrom, & Freel, 1997).

As our consideration of the importance of balancing comforting and challenging contexts indicated, all contexts cannot and should not be oriented to maximizing comfort. There are clear developmental benefits in being exposed to challenges and demands that evoke high levels of engagement, problem solving, and the acquisition of coping skills. However, as Simmons and Blyth (1987) recognized, contexts that provide these experiences must be offset by those offering solace and support.

Furthermore, our results indicate that to obtain an ameliorative influence, it may not always be necessary to alter those contexts that are the most immediate determinants of adolescent distress. Given that people are likely to extricate themselves from distressful situations when they are able to do so, the presence of persistent chronic strain in an environment may indicate its essentially nondiscretionary, even coercive, character. For example, early and middle adolescents are required to attend school and are thereby subject to the particular transitions from one school to another, institutionalized in a given community, that are often found to be stressful (Eccles et al., 1997). Although school transitions might be timed in a manner more conducive to adolescent adjustment (Simmons & Blyth, 1987), central aspects of education that engender distress (e.g., grading) are not readily altered.

Moreover, although some adolescents decide to leave stressful home environments, this is a rather drastic action that gives rise to a host of new difficulties. Potentially stressful environments, such as the family, may also present long-term strains (e.g., parental mental illness) that are relatively impervious to external manipulation.

Although certain features of adolescent contexts are, from the perspective of intervention, relatively fixed, others are potentially manipulatable. If the findings of this research are correct, attention might be turned to a variety of arenas. Adolescents may be encouraged to select or construct more comforting contexts; some contexts may be improved directly by ameliorative interventions. The negative sequelae of another, essentially discomforting context may thus be avoided. For example, students who are having difficulties in their families can be encouraged in mentoring programs to develop a supportive relationship with a caring adult, be it a supervisor at work, a teacher, or another person. Comfortable experiences might also be provided by community organizations, sports teams, and social clubs, as well as by youth organizations linked to religious institutions. Given the diverse institutions and groups that are accessible to adolescents, the opportunities for offering supportive, comforting environments are indeed manifold.

This does not mean to say that interventions should not be targeted to individual adolescents. If, in fact, persons are continually developing and constructing the very environments that affect the course of their further development, it becomes essential to enhance whatever competencies are necessary to do this in an effective manner. In view of the importance of adolescent agency in selecting and constructing supportive relationships with others, interventions should be designed to improve self-presentation, communication, constructive expression of negative feelings, and other interpersonal skills. Diminishing adolescents' tendencies to withdraw from, avoid, distrust, or otherwise deter the formation of relationships with potentially supportive others would likely also yield important contextual benefits.

Moreover, Petersen et al. (1997) provided evidence that an intervention to increase adolescents' "awareness of different areas of life (e.g., friends, family, school) and importance of using strengths when challenges in other areas are causing stress" (p. 483) was successful in improving mastery and coping skills. If adolescents are made aware of the importance of alternating support and challenge in their environments, they may become more capable in constructing a developmentally beneficial mix.

What directions are suggested by this study for further research? First, although Simmons (in press) implied a close connection between contextual change and feelings of discomfort, the relationship between objective change and subjective discomfort remains problematic. Contrary to this hypothesis, chapter 5 reports that changes in the family did not affect perceptions of discomfort in parent–child relations. It may be that, for most adolescents, relations with mothers and fathers are relatively stable and not readily disrupted even in the face of moving, new additions to the family, unemployment, and similar changes. In comparison to the changes assessed by Simmons and her colleagues (Simmons & Blyth, 1987; Simmons et al., 1987)—school transitions, onset of puberty, and initiation of dating—those measured in the present study may not be as directly salient to adolescents' adjustment or identity, and therefore not as directly linked to feelings of discomfort.

If, in fact, changes in a given setting do not engender feelings of discomfort in that setting, it could reasonably be inferred that a changing context could still function as an arena of comfort. Moreover, if a context remains stable, yet the individual does not judge it to be a supportive, comfortable setting, it would not qualify as such an arena. Perceptions of comfort may thus be more critical than the objective events that occur in a particular setting (Merriam & Clark, 1993). Further investigation needs to clarify the criteria that make a context effective as an arena of comfort. Perhaps those contexts that have the strongest comforting and, therefore, buffering capacity are those that involve both perceived comfort and an absence of change.

Second, we have not directly investigated a key component of Simmons and Blyth's (1987) hypothetical structure: that comfort deriving from an external source is more powerful in its capacity to act as a moderator of stress than that found within a particular stressor setting. As noted in chapter 5, one would need to have access to measures of social support both within and outside particular stressor settings to adequately evaluate this key contention. That is, support received from siblings or a live-in grandparent could possibly effectively moderate the negative consequences of problematic parent–adolescent relationships.

Third, the important issue of identity salience could not be addressed in this research. Simmons and colleagues (Simmons, in press; Simmons & Blyth, 1987) hypothesized that some contexts or role-relationships are more important to the individual's self-image and self-comfort, and thereby more significant in the stress process. The degree of commitment or psychological engagement in associated roles may be an important determinant of the relative discomfort accompanying change in a particular context. That is, it may be more difficult for a person to deal with change or discomfort in an arena in which the person is heavily involved and psychologically invested (Stryker, 1980; Thoits, 1983). By the same token, the high salience of a domain could enhance its power to influence mental health as well as its capacity to act as a moderator of stressors encountered elsewhere. The implications of identity salience or role commitment for adolescent development, as well as for cross-domain buffering processes, deserve further attention.

Fourth, our attempt to operationalize the arena of comfort construct raised a host of issues that call for additional study. This construct originated as a post hoc explanatory tool in the work of Simmons and her associates and was therefore not intentionally measured (Simmons & Blyth, 1987; Simmons et al., 1987). Indicators of perceived social support, satisfaction, and low levels of stress, which are captured by our operationalization, are justified by their conceptualization. Still other pertinent components have not been appropriately addressed.

Support and the absence of stress are central ingredients to the construct, but Simmons' (in press) conceptualization of the comfort arena goes well beyond them. An arena of comfort encompasses diverse evaluative, affective, and cognitive components. The evaluative element emphasized in this research involves the individual's appraisal of whether relationships and experiences are satisfying or supportive. The affective component of a comfort arena involves moderate arousal and feelings of calmness and ease. The person is not on stage or being evaluated by others. Finally, the cognitive aspect of the arena of comfort implies an awareness of the experiences and role-relationships that will be encountered within that context—their unambiguous, predictable nature. In the words of Merriam and Clark (1993), an arena of comfort is an "internal reality," a context that is perceived as consistent and affirming. It is a sure thing.

The evaluative component of comfort has been addressed most fully by our measurement of perceived social support in family, school, peer, and work settings. However, in addition to appraisals of relationships as warm and accepting, the openness of interpersonal communication would appear to be particularly germane (Bradbury & Fincham, 1990). Additional indicators might tap the degree of mutual understanding among family, friends, coworkers, or other role partners.

Measures of attachment would also be useful, assessing the bond between adolescents and their parents or people outside their family. Brethertin, Biringen, and Ridgeway (1991) described attachment relationships or experiences as responsive to distressing situations, providing "reassurance, comfort, and protection (secure haven)" (p. 1). Rathunde and Csikszentmihalyi (1991) associated attachment between parents and adolescents with integration among family members. Integration entails strong and satisfying relations fostered by working toward mutual goals and thereby perpetuating family traditions, values, and beliefs. Adolescents could be queried about their degree of investment in the relationships, goals, and activities in particular contexts.

Concerning the affective component of a comfort arena, one could ask people directly whether they feel that they can act like themselves in particular settings without worrying about what others think of them. Measures of emotional arousal in particular contexts could also be included. When referring to self-comfort, Simmons (in press) stressed the importance of moderate emotion states—that is, feeling happy, calm, and tranquil, as opposed to the emotional extremes of exhilaration, stress, or boredom. Is comfort in the family arena so consequential to well-being because it acts as a "balance wheel in the emotional swings of adolescent life" (Csikszentmihalyi & Larson, 1984, p. 134), providing a hiatus from the emotional highs and lows experienced at school and with friends?

The cognitive aspect of an arena of comfort pertains to predictability and trust. For example, sustained routines and activities engender a sense of security, stability, and trust. Items reflecting the belief that other people are dependable, reliable, and responsive in meeting one's needs (Berscheid, 1994) would be especially useful.

Finally, it would be most instructive to elicit adolescents' own rankings of the comfort they experience in particular settings. As we often reminded the reader, the fact that our measures of comfort across settings are not the same renders our comparisons somewhat suspect. We concluded, for example, based on indicators of social support in each setting, that when the contexts are considered one at a time, most adolescents find comfort in the family (especially with mothers), in peer relations, and at school. If asked to compare them directly, however, a rank ordering may be much more prominent. Investigation of the phenomenological experience of comfort would illuminate the processes through which it enhances the self-image by encouraging a perception of self as worthy, competent, and authentic (Gecas, 1986), promoting mental health and enabling the adolescent to cope with challenge and adversity.

It could be argued that comfort has meaning well beyond its gratifying, rejuvenating, and stress-reducing impacts that play such an important part in Simmons and her colleagues' analysis (Simmons & Blyth, 1987; Simmons et al., 1987). The capacity to find comfort across a diversity of arenas in the life space may have important symbolic significance, signifying to adolescents, as well as their parents and various other significant others, that the young person is successfully moving toward a new, more mature adult status. That is, the capacity to develop positive social relationships with persons outside the family sphere, including peers, teachers, and supervisors at work, denotes successful expansion of the maturing adolescent's social world. Finding satisfaction and a lack of distress in the more achievement-oriented, instrumental spheres of school and work-place may be especially perceived as auguring future success in the adult occupational world.

Adequate functioning across a variety of life arenas is a well-recognized necessity of adulthood in modern differentiated societies. Thus, finding comfort, gratification, and a sense of accomplishment across a variety of arenas could engender cognitive attributions and interpretations that foster a sense of competence, self-esteem, and psychological well-being. Demonstrating the capacity to find satisfaction across multiple domains of adolescent life could reduce the likelihood of fearful ruminations and negative anticipations of the future and evoke confidence in dealing with the approaching challenges of adulthood. Clearly, we have much to learn about the processes through which arenas of comfort promote mental health, resilience, and behavioral adjustment in adolescence.

References

Allgood-Merten, B., Lewinsohn, P. M., & Hops, H. (1990). Sex differences and depression. *Journal of Abnormal Psychology, 99,* 55–63.

Aronson, P. J., Mortimer, J. T., Zierman, C., & Hacker, M. (1996). Generational differences in early work experience and evaluations. In J. T. Mortimer & M. D. Finch (Eds.), *Adolescents, work, and family* (pp. 25–62). Thousand Oaks, CA: Sage.

Bachman, J. G. (1970). *Youth in transition: Vol. II. The impact of family background and intelligence on tenth-grade boys.* Ann Arbor, MI: Survey Research Center, Institute for Social Research.

Baldwin, A. L., Baldwin, C., & Cole, R. E. (1990). Stress-resistant families and stress-resistant children. In J. Rolf, A. S. Masten, D. Cicchetti, K. H. Nuechterlein, & S. Weintraub (Eds.), *Risk and protective factors in the development of psychopathology* (pp. 257–280). New York: Cambridge University Press.

Bandura, A. (1977). Self-efficacy: Toward a unifying theory of behavioral change. *Psychological Review, 84,* 191–215.

Bandura, A. (1986). *Social foundations of thought and action: A social cognitive theory.* Englewood Cliffs, NJ: Prentice-Hall.

Bandura, A. (1997). *Self-efficacy. The exercise of control.* New York: W. H. Freeman.

Barber, B. K., & Thomas, D. L. (1986). Dimensions of fathers' and mothers' supportive behavior: The case for physical affection. *Journal of Marriage and the Family, 48,* 783–794.

Baron, R. M., & Kenny, D. A. (1986). The moderator-mediator variable distinction in social psychological research: Conceptual, strategic, and statistical considerations. *Journal of Personality and Social Psychology, 51,* 1173–1182.

Baumrind, D. (1987). A developmental perspective on adolescent risk-taking behavior in contemporary America. In W. Damon (Ed.), *New directions for child development: Adolescent health and social behavior* (Vol. 37, pp. 92–126). San Francisco, CA: Jossey-Bass.

Berscheid, E. (1994). Interpersonal relationships. *Annual Review of Psychology, 45,* 79–129.

Bielby, D. D. (1992). Commitment to work and family. *Annual Review of Sociology, 18,* 281–302.

Blalock, H. M., Jr. (1972). *Social statistics* (2nd ed.). New York: McGraw-Hill.

Bleuler, M. (1978). *The schizophrenic disorders: Long-term patient and family studies*. New Haven, CT: Yale University Press.

Bolger, N., DeLongis, A., Kessler, R. C., & Wethington, E. (1989). The contagion of stress across multiple roles. *Journal of Marriage and the Family, 51,* 175–183.

Bradbury, T. N., & Fincham, F. D. (1990). Dimensions of marital and family interaction. In J. Touliatos, B. F. Perlmutter, & M. A. Straus (Eds.), *Handbook of family measurement techniques* (pp. 37–60). Newbury Park, CA: Sage.

Brandstaedter, J. (1998). Action perspectives on human development. In R. M. Lerner (Ed.), *Handbook of child psychology. Theoretical models of human development* (Vol. 1, pp. 807–863). New York: Wiley.

Bretherton, I., Biringen, Z., & Ridgeway, D. (1991). The parental side of attachment. In K. Pillemer & K. McCartney (Eds.), *Parent–child relations throughout life* (pp. 1–24). Hillsdale, NJ: Lawrence Erlbaum Associates.

Bronfenbrenner, U. (1979). *The ecology of human development: Experiments by nature and design*. Cambridge, MA: Harvard University Press.

Bronfenbrenner, U. (1986). Recent advances in research on the ecology of human development. In R. K. Silbereisen, K. Eyferth, & G. Rudinger (Eds.), *Development as action in context* (pp. 287–310). New York: Springer-Verlag.

Brooks-Gunn, J. (1991). How stressful is the transition to adolescence for girls? In M. E. Colten & S. Gore (Eds.), *Adolescent stress: Causes and consequences* (pp. 131–149). Hawthorne, NY: Aldine de Gruyter.

Brown, B. B. (1990). Peer groups and peer cultures. In S. S. Feldman & G. R. Elliott (Eds.), *At the threshold: The developing adolescent* (pp. 171–196). Cambridge, MA: Harvard University Press.

Brown, B. B., Dolcini, M. M., & Leventhal, A. (1997). Transformations in peer relationships at adolescence: Implications for health-related behavior. In J. Schulenberg, J. M. Maggs, & K. Hurrelmann (Eds.), *Health risks and developmental transitions during adolescence* (pp. 161–189). Cambridge, England: Cambridge University Press.

Brown, B. B., Eicher, S. A., & Pertie, S. (1986). The importance of peer group ("crowd") affiliation in adolescence. *Journal of Adolescence, 9,* 73–96.

Bukowski, W. M., Newcomb, A. F., & Hoza, B. (1987). Friendships conceptions among early adolescents: A longitudinal study of stability and change. *Journal of Early Adolescence, 7,* 143–152.

Burton, R. P. D. (1998). Global integrative meaning as a mediating factor in the relationship between social roles and psychological distress. *Journal of Health and Social Behavior, 39,* 201–215.

Bush, D. M., & Simmons, R. G. (1987). Gender and coping with entry into early adolescence. In R. C. Barnett, L. Breiner, & G. Baruch (Eds.), *Gender and stress* (pp. 185–217). New York: The Free Press.

Cairns, R. B., Cairns, B. D., Rodkin, P., & Xie, H. (1998). New directions in developmental research: Models and methods. In R. Jessor (Ed.), *New perspectives on adolescent risk behavior* (pp. 13–40). Cambridge, England: Cambridge University Press.

Call, K. T. (1996). Implications of helpfulness for possible selves. In J. T. Mortimer & M. D. Finch (Eds.), *Adolescents, work, and family: An intergenerational developmental analysis* (pp. 63–96). Newbury Park, CA: Sage.

Call, K. T., Mortimer, J. T., & Shanahan, M. J. (1995). Helpfulness and the development of competence in adolescence. *Child Development, 66,* 129–138.

Call, K. T., & McNall, M. (1992). Poverty, ethnicity, youth adjustment: A comparison of poor Hmong and non-Hmong adolescents. In W. Meeus, M. de Goede, W. Kox, & K. Hurrelmann (Eds.), *Adolescence, careers and cultures* (pp. 373–392). Berlin, New York: W. de Gruyter.

Caspi, A., & Moffitt, T. E. (1995). The continuity of adaptive behavior. In D. Cicchettti & D. J. Cohen (Eds.), *Developmental psychopathology. Risk, disorder, and adaptation* (Vol. 2, pp. 472–511). New York: Wiley.

Cauce, A. M., Felner, R. D., & Primavera, J. (1982). Social support in high-risk adolescents: Structural components and adaptive impact. *American Journal of Community Psychology, 10,* 417–428.

Cicchetti, D., & Toth, S. L. (1995). Developmental psychopathology and disorder of affect. In D. Cicchetti & D. J. Cohen (Eds.), *Developmental psychopathology. Risk, disorder, and adaptation* (Vol. 2, pp. 369–420). New York: Wiley.

Clark, R. (1983). *Family life and school achievement: Why poor black children succeed or fail.* Chicago, IL: University of Chicago Press.

Cohen, S., & Wills, T. A. (1985). Stress, social support, and the buffering hypothesis. *Psychological Bulletin, 98,* 310–357.

Coleman, J. C. (1974). *Relationships in adolescence.* Boston, MA: Routledge & P. Kegan.

Coleman, J. S. (1961). *The adolescent society.* New York: The Free Press.

Committee on the Health and Safety Implications of Child Labor. (1998). *Protecting youth at work. Health, safety, and development of working children and adolescents in the United States.* Washington, DC: National Academy Press.

Compas, B. E. (1987). Coping with stress during childhood and adolescence. *Psychological Bulletin, 101,* 393–403.

Compas, B. E., Connor, J. K., & Hinden, B. R. (1998). New perspectives on depression during adolescence. In R. Jessor (Ed.), *New perspectives on adolescent risk behavior* (pp. 319–362). Cambridge, England: Cambridge University Press.

Compas, B. E., Davis, G. E., Forsythe, C. J., & Wagner, B. M. (1986). Assessment of major and daily stressful events during adolescence: The adolescent perceived events scale. *Journal of Consulting and Clinical Psychology, 55,* 534–541.

Compas, B. E., & Hammen, C. L. (1996). Child and adolescent depression: Covariation and comorbidity in development. In R. J. Haggerty, L. R. Sherrod, N. Garmezy, & M. Rutter (Eds.), *Stress, risk and resilience in children and adolescents: Process, mechanisms, and interventions* (pp. 225–267). Cambridge, England: Cambridge University Press.

Compas, B. E., Slavin, L. A., Wagner, B. M., & Vannatta, K. (1986). Relationship of life events and social support with psychological dysfunction among adolescents. *Journal of Youth and Adolescence, 15,* 203–219.

Crockett, L. J. (1997). Cultural, historical and subcultural contexts of adolescence: Implications for health and development. In J. Schulenberg, M.J. Maggs, & K. Hurrelmann (Eds.), *Health risks and developmental transitions during adolescence* (pp. 23–53). Cambridge, England: Cambridge University Press.

Cronbach, L. J. (1987). Statistical tests for moderator variables: Flaws in analyses recently proposed. *Psychological Bulletin, 102,* 114–117.

Csikszentmihalyi, M., & Larson, R. (1984). *Being adolescent: Conflict and growth in the teenage years.* New York: Basic Books.

Delongis, A., Coyne, J. C., Dakof, G., Folkman, S., & Lazarus, R. S. (1982). Relationships of hassles, uplifts, and major life events to health status. *Health Psychology, 1,* 119–136.

Demo, D. H., & Acock, A. C. (1988). The impact of divorce on children. *Journal of Marriage and the Family, 50,* 619–648.

Dillman, D. A. (1983). Mail and other self-administered questionnaires. In P. H. Rossi, J. D. Wright, & A. B. Anderson (Eds.), *Handbook of survey research* (pp. 359–377). New York: Academic Press.

Dornbusch, S. M., Mont-Reynaud, R., Ritter, P. L., Chen, Z., & Steinberg, L. (1991). Stressful events and their correlates among adolescents from diverse backgrounds. In M. E. Colten & S. Gore (Eds.), *Adolescent stress: Causes and consequences* (pp. 111–130). Hawthorne, NY: Aldine de Gruyter.

Dornbusch, S. M., Ritter, P. L., Leiderman, P. H., Roberts, D. F., & Fraleigh, M. J. (1987). The relation of parenting style to adolescent school performance. *Child Development, 58,* 1244–1257.

Douvan, E., & Adelson, J. (1966). *The adolescent experience.* New York: Wiley.

Dreeben, R. (1968). *On what is learned in school reading.* Reading, MA: Addison-Wesley.

Ebata, A. T., Petersen, A. C., & Conger, J. J. (1990). The development of psychopathology in adolescence. In J. Rolf, A. S. Masten, D. Cicchetti, K. H. Nuechterlein, & S. Weintraub (Eds.), *Risk and protective factors in the development of psychopathology* (pp. 308–333). New York: Cambridge University Press.

Eccles, J. S., Lord, S. E., Roeser, R. W., Barber, B. L., & Jozefowicz, D. M. H. (1997). The association of school transitions in early adolescence with developmental trajectories through high school. In J. Schulenberg, J. M. Maggs, & K. Hurrelmann (Eds.), *Health risks and developmental transitions during adolescence* (pp. 283–320). Cambridge, England: Cambridge University Press.

Eckenrode, J., & Gore, S. (1990). *Stress between work and family.* New York: Plenum.

Elder, G. H., Jr. (1974). *Children of the great depression: Social change and life experience.* Chicago, IL: University of Chicago Press.

Elder, G. H., Jr., Caspi, A., & Van Nguyen, T. (1986). Resourceful and vulnerable children: Family influences in hard times. In R. K. Silbereisen, K. Eyferth, & G. Rudinger (Eds.), *Development as action in context* (pp. 167–186). Berlin: Springer-Verlag.

Elder, G. H., Jr., Van Nguyen, T., & Caspi, A. (1985). Linking family hardship to children's life. *Child Development, 56,* 361–375.

Elliott, D. S., & Voss, H. L. (1974). *Delinquency and dropout.* Lexington, MS: Lexington Books.

Emery, R. E. (1988). *Marriage, divorce, and children's adjustment.* Beverly Hills, CA: Sage.

Emery, R. E., & Kitzmann, K. M. (1995). The child in the family: Disruptions in family functions. In D. Cicchetti & D. J. Cohen (Eds.), *Developmental psychopathology. Risk, disorder, and adaptation* (Vol. 2, pp. 3–31). New York: Wiley.

Entwisle, D. R. (1990). Schools and the adolescent. In S. S. Feldman & G. R. Elliott (Eds.), *At the threshold: The developing adolescent* (pp. 197–224). Cambridge, MA: Harvard University Press.

Erikson, E. H. (1968). *Identity, youth, and crisis.* New York: Norton.

Feldman, S. S., & Elliott, G. R. (Eds.). (1990). *At the threshold: The developing adolescent.* Cambridge, MA: Harvard University Press.

Felice, L. (1981). Black student dropout behavior: Disengagement from school, rejection and racial discrimination. *The Journal of Negro Education, 50,* 415–424.

Finch, M. D., Shanahan, M. J., Mortimer, J. T., & Ryu, S. (1991). Work experience and control orientation in adolescence. *American Sociological Review, 56,* 596–611.

Fine, M., & Rosenberg, P. (1983). Dropping out of high school: The ideology of school and work. *Journal of Education, 165,* 257–272.

Furstenberg, F. F., Jr. (1981). *National survey of children (Wave II).* Philadelphia, PA: Institute for Social Research, Temple University.

Furstenberg, F. F., Jr. (1987). The new extended family: The experience of parents and children after remarriage. In K. Pasley & M. Inenger-Tallman (Eds.), *Remarriage and stepparenting: Current research and theory* (pp. 42–61). New York: Guilford.

Furstenberg, F. F., Jr. (1988). Child care after divorce and remarriage. In E. M. Hetherington & J. D. Arasteh (Eds.), *Impact of divorce, single parenting, and stepparenting on children* (pp. 245–261). Hillsdale, NJ: Lawrence Erlbaum Associates.

Galambos, N. L., & Ehrenberg, M. F. (1997). The family as health risk and opportunity: A focus on divorce and working families. In J. Schulenberg, J. M. Maggs, & K. Hurrelmann (Eds.), *Health risks and developmental transitions during adolescence* (pp. 139–160). Cambridge, England: Cambridge University Press.

Galambos, N. L., Sears, H. A., Almeida, D. M., & Kolaric, G. C. (1995). Parents' work overload and problem behavior in young adolescents. *Journal of Research on Adolescence, 5,* 201–223.

Garbarino, J. (1992). The meaning of poverty in the world of children. *American Behavioral Scientist, 35,* 220–237.

Garmezy, N. (1985). Stress-resistent children: The search for protective factors. In J. E. Stevenson (Ed.), *Recent research in developmental psychopathology* (pp. 213–234). New York: Pergamon.

Garmezy, N. (1987). Stress, competence, and development: Continuities in the study of schizophrenic adults, children vulnerable to psychopathology, and the search for stress-resistant children. *American Journal of Orthopsychiatry, 57,* 159–174.

Ge, X., Lorenz, F. O., Conger, R. D., Elder, G. H., & Simons, R. L. (1994). Trajectories of stressful life events and depressive symptoms during adolescence. *Developmental Psychology, 30,* 467–483.

Gecas, V. (1979). The influence of social class on socialization. In W. R. Burr, R. Hill, L. Reiss, & F. I. Nye (Eds.), *Contemporary theories about the family* (pp. 365–404). New York: The Free Press.

Gecas, V. (1986). The motivational significance of self-concept for socialization theory. *Advances in Group Processes, 3,* 131–156.

Gecas, V. (1989). The social psychology of self-efficacy. *Annual Review of Sociology, 15,* 291–316.

Gecas, V., & Seff, M. A. (1989). Social class, occupational conditions, and self-esteem. *Sociological Perspectives, 32,* 353–365.

Gecas, V., & Seff, M. A. (1990). Social class and self-esteem: Psychological centrality, compensation, and the relative effects of work and home. *Social Psychology Quarterly, 53,* 165–173.

Gecas, V., & Seff, M. A. (1991). Families and adolescents: A review of the 1980s. In A. Booth (Ed.), *Contemporary families: Looking forward, looking back* (pp. 208–225). Minneapolis, MN: National Council on Family Relations.

Gilligan, C. (1982). *In a different voice.* Cambridge, MA: Harvard University Press.

Gore, S., & Colten, M. E. (1991). Introduction: Adolescent stress, social relationships, and mental health. In M. E. Colten & S. Gore (Eds.), *Adolescent stress: Causes and consequences* (pp. 1–14). Hawthorne, NY: Aldine de Gruyter.

Greenberger, E. (1988). Working in teenage America. In J. T. Mortimer & K. M. Borman (Eds.), *Work experience and psychological development through the life span* (pp. 21–50). Boulder, CO: Westview.

Greenberger, E., & Steinberg, L. D. (1986). *When teenagers work: The psychological and social costs of adolescent employment.* New York: Basic Books.

Hartup, W. W. (1983). Peer relations. In P. H. Mussen (Ed.), *Handbook of child psychology. Socialization* (Vol. 4, pp. 103–196). New York: Wiley.

Hauser, S. T., & Bowlds, M. K. (1990). Stress coping and adaptation. In S. S. Feldman & G. R. Elliott (Eds.), *At the threshold: The developing adolescent* (pp. 388–413). Cambridge, MA: Harvard University Press.

Henderson, S., Byrne, D., Duncan-Jones, P., Scott, R., & Adcock, S. (1980). Social relationships, adversity, and neurosis: A study of associations in a general population sample. *British Journal of Psychiatry, 136,* 574–583.

Hendrix, B. L. (1980). The effects of locus of control on the self-esteem of black and white youth. *The Journal of Psychology, 112,* 301–302.

Hetherington, E. M. (1989). Coping with family transitions: Winners, losers, and survivors. *Child Development, 60,* 1–14.

Hetherington, E. M., Cox, M., & Cox, R. (1985). Long-term effects of divorce and remarriage on the adjustment of children. *Journal of the American Academy of Child Psychiatry, 24,* 518–530.

Hirsch, B. J., & Rapkin, B. D. (1986). Multiple roles, social networks, and women's well-being. *Journal of Personality and Social Psychology, 51*, 1237–1247.

House, J. S., Landis, K. R., & Umberson, D. (1988). Social relationships and health. *Science, 241*, 540–545.

House, J. S., & Mortimer, J. T. (1990). Social structure and the individual: Emerging themes and new directions. *Social Psychology Quarterly, 53*, 71–80.

Jackson, S., & Rodriguez-Tome, H. (1993). *Adolescence and its social worlds*. Hillsdale, NJ: Lawrence Erlbaum Associates.

Jessor, R., & Jessor, S. L. (1977). *Problem behavior and psychosocial development: A longitudinal study of youth*. San Diego, CA: Academic Press.

Johnson, M. K., & Mortimer, J. T. (2000). Work-family orientations and attainments in the early life course. In T. L. Parcel & D. B. Cornfield (Eds.), *Work and family: Research informing policy* (pp. 215–248). Thousand Oaks, CA: Sage.

Kandel, D. B. (1978). Homophily, selection, and socialization in adolescent friendships. *American Journal of Sociology, 84*, 427–436.

Kandel, D. B., Davies, M., & Raveis, V. H. (1985). The stressfulness of daily social roles for women: Marital, occupational and household roles. *Journal of Health and Social Behavior, 26*, 64–78.

Kessler, R. C., & McLeod, J. D. (1985). Social support and mental health in community samples. In S. S. Cohen (Ed.), *Social support and health* (pp. 219–240). Orlando, FL: Academic Press.

Kessler, R. C., & Neighbors, H. W. (1986). A new perspective on the relationships among race, social class, and psychological distress. *Journal of Health and Social Behavior, 27*, 107–115.

Kohn, M. L., & Schooler, C. (1973). Occupational experience and psychological functioning: An assessment of reciprocal effects. *American Sociological Review, 38*, 97–118.

Kohn, M. L., & Schooler, C. (1974a). *Study of occupations (adult version)*. Chicago, IL: National Opinion Research Center, University of Chicago.

Kohn, M. L., & Schooler, C. (1974b). *Study of occupations (child version)*. Chicago, IL: National Opinion Research Center, University of Chicago.

Kohn, M. L., Schooler, C., Miller, J., Miller, K. A., Schoenbach, C., & Schoenberg, R. (1983). *Work and personality: An inquiry into the impact of social stratification*. Norwood, NJ: Ablex.

Larson, R., & Asmussen, L. (1991). Anger, worry, and hurt in early adolescence: An enlarging world of negative emotions. In M. E. Colten & S. Gore (Eds.), *Adolescent stress: Causes and consequences* (pp. 21–41). Hawthorne, NY: Aldine de Gruyter.

Lasch, C. (1977). *Haven in a heartless world: The family besieged*. New York: Basic Books.

Lazarus, R. S., & Folkman, S. (1984). *Stress, appraisal, and coping*. New York: Springer.

LeCroy, C. W. (1989). Parent-adolescent intimacy: Impact on adolescent functioning. *Adolescence, 23*, 137–147.

Lempers, J. D., Clark-Lempers, D., & Simons, R. L. (1989). Economic hardship parenting, and distress in adolescence. *Child Development, 60*, 25–39.

Lepore, S. J. (1992). Social conflict, social support, and psychological distress: Evidence of cross-domain buffering effects. *Journal of Personality and Social Psychology, 63*, 857–867.

Lerner, R. M. (1985). Individual and context in developmental psychology: Conceptual and theoretical issues. In J. R. Nesselroade & A. von Eye (Eds.), *Individual development and social change: Explanatory analysis* (pp. 155–187). New York: Academic Press.

Lerner, R. M., Ostrom, C. W., & Freel, M. A. (1997). Preventing health-compromising behaviors among youth and promoting their positive development: A developmental contextual perspective. In J. Schulenberg, J. M. Maggs, & K. Hurelmann (Eds.), *Health risks and developmental transitions during adolescence* (pp. 498–521). Cambridge, England: Cambridge University Press.

Liem, J. H., & Liem, G. R. (1990). Understanding the individual and family effects of unemployment. In J. Eckenrode & S. Gore (Eds.), *Stress between work and family* (pp. 175–204). New York: Plenum.

Linville, P. W. (1985). Self complexity and affective extremity: Don't put all of your eggs in one cognitive basket. *Social Cognition, 3*, 94–120.

Lowenthal, M., Thurnher, M., & Chiriboga, D. (1975). *Four stages of life*. San Francisco, CA: Jossey-Bass.

Luthar, S. S. (1991). Vulnerability and resilience: A study of high-risk adolescents. *Child Development, 62*, 600–616.

Maccoby, E. E. (1983). Social-emotional development and response to stressors. In N. Garmezy & M. Rutter (Eds.), *Stress, coping, and development in children* (pp. 217–234). New York: McGraw-Hill.

Maccoby, E. E., & Jacklin, C. N. (1974). *The psychology of sex differences*. Stanford, CA: Stanford University Press.

Maccoby, E. E., & Martin, J. (1983). Socialization in the context of the family: Parent–child interaction. In E. M. Hetherington (Ed.), *Handbook of child psychology: Socialization, personality and social development* (Vol. 4, pp. 1–101). New York: Wiley.

Maggs, J. L. (1997). Alcohol use and binge drinking as goal-directed action during the transition to postsecondary education. In J. Schulenberg, J. M. Maggs, & K. Hurrelmann (Eds.) *Health risks and developmental transitions during adolescence* (pp. 345–371). Cambridge, England: Cambridge University Press.

Maggs, J. L., Schulenberg, J., & Hurrelmann, K. (1997). Developmental transitions during adolescence: Health promotion implications. In J. Schulenberg, J. M. Maggs, & K. Hurrelmann (Eds.), *Health risks and developmental transitions during adolescence* (pp. 522–546). Cambridge, England: Cambridge University Press.

Manning, W. D. (1990). Parenting employed teenagers. *Youth and Society, 22*, 184–200.

Markus, H., Cross, S., & Wurf, E. (1990). The role of the self-system in competence. In R. J. Steinberg & J. Kolligan, Jr. (Eds.), *Competence considered* (pp. 205–226). New Haven, CT: Yale University Press.

Masten, A. S., & Braswell, L. (1991). Developmental psychopathology: An integrative framework for understanding behavior problems in children and adolescents. In P. R. Martin (Ed.), *Handbook of behavior therapy and psychological science: An integrative approach* (pp. 35–56). New York: Pergamon.

Masten, A. S., & Coatsworth, J. D. (1995). Competence, resilience, and psychopathology. In D. Cicchetti & D. J. Cohen (Eds.), *Developmental psychopathology. Risk, disorder, and adaptation* (Vol. 2, pp. 715–752). New York: Wiley.

Masten, A. S., & Garmezy, N. (1985). Risk, vulnerability, and protective factors in developmental psychopathology. In B. B. Lahey & A. E. Kazdin (Eds.), *Advances in clinical child psychology* (Vol. VIII, pp. 1–52). New York: Plenum.

McLeod, J. D., & Kessler, R. C. (1990). Socioeconomic status differences in vulnerability to undesirable life events. *Journal of Health and Social Behavior, 31*, 162–172.

McLoyd, V. C. (1990). The impact of economic hardship on black families and children: Psychological distress, parenting, and socioemotional development. *Child Development, 61*, 311–346.

Menaghan, E. G. (1990). Social stress and individual distress. *Research in Community and Mental Health, 6*, 107–141.

Merriam, S. B., & Clark, M. C. (1993). Work and love: Their relationship in adulthood. *International Journal of Behavioral Development, 16*, 609–627.

Merton, R. K. (1968). *Social theory and social structure*. New York: The Free Press.

Mirowsky, J., & Ross, C. E. (1980). Minority status, ethnic culture, and distress: A comparison of blacks, whites, Mexicans, and Mexican Americans. *American Journal of Sociology, 86,* 479–495.

Mortimer, J. T. (Ed.). (1994). Individual differences as precursors of unemployment. In *Youth unemployment and society* (pp. 172–198). New York: Cambridge University Press.

Mortimer, J. T., & Finch, M. D. (Eds.). (1996). *Adolescents, work and family: An intergenerational developmental analysis.* Thousand Oaks, CA: Sage.

Mortimer, J. T., Finch, M. D., Dennehy, K., Lee, C., & Beebe, T. (1994). Work experience in adolescence. *Journal of Vocational Education Research, 19,* 39–70.

Mortimer, J. T., Finch, M. D., Owens, T. J., & Shanahan, M. J. (1990). Gender and work in adolescence. *Youth and Society, 22,* 201–224.

Mortimer, J. T., Finch, M. J., Shanahan, M. J., & Ryu, S. (1992a). Work experience, mental health, and behavioral adjustment in adolescence. *Journal of Research on Adolescence, 2,* 25–57.

Mortimer, J. T., Finch, M. J., Shanahan, M. J., & Ryu, S. (1992b). Adolescent work history behavioral adjustment. *Journal of Research on Adolescence, 2,* 59–80.

Mortimer, J. T., & Johnson, M.K. (1998). New perspectives on adolesent work and the transition to adulthood. In R. Jessor (Ed.), *New perspectives on adolescent risk behavior* (pp. 425–496). Cambridge, England: Cambridge University Press.

Mortimer, J. T., & Lorence, J. (1979a). Work experience and occupational value socialization: A longitudinal study. *American Journal of Sociology, 84,* 1361–1385.

Mortimer, J. T., & Lorence, J. (1979b). Occupational experience and the self-concept: A longitudinal study. *Social Psychology Quarterly, 42,* 307–323.

Mortimer, J. T., Lorence, J., & Kumka, D. (1986). *Work, family and personality: Transition to adulthood.* Norwood, NJ: Ablex.

Mortimer, J. T., Pimentel, E., Ryu, S., Nash, K., & Lee, C. (1996). Part-time work and occupational value formation in adolescence. *Social Forces, 74,* 1405–1418.

Mortimer, J. T., & Shanahan, M. J. (1994). Adolescent work experience and family relationships. *Work and Occupations, 21,* 369–384.

Murphy, L. B., & Moriarty, A. E. (1976). *Vulnerability, coping, and growth: From infancy to adolescence.* New Haven, CT: Yale University Press.

Nettles, S. M., & Pleck, J. H. (1996). Risk, resilience, and development: The multiple ecologies of black adolescents in the United States. In R. J. Haggerty, L. R. Sherrod, N. Garmezy, & M. Rutter (Eds.), *Stress, risk, and resilience in children and adolescents. Processes, mechanisms, and interventions* (pp. 147–181). Cambridge, England: Cambridge University Press.

Nidorf, J. F. (1985). Mental health and refugee youths: A model for diagnostic training. In T. C. Owen (Ed.), *Southeast Asian mental health: Treatment, prevention, services, training, and research* (pp. 319–327). Washington, DC: National Institute for Mental Health.

Noack, P., & Kracke, B. (1997). Social change and adolescent well-being: Healthy country, healthy teens. In J. Schulenberg, J. M. Maggs, & K. Hurrelmann (Eds.), *Health risks and developmental transitions during adolescence* (pp. 54–84). Cambridge, England: Cambridge University Press.

Nurmi, J.-E. (1993). Adolescent development in an age-graded context: The role of personal beliefs, goals, and strategies in the tackling of developmental tasks and standards. *International Journal of Behavioral Development, 16,* 169–189.

Nurmi, J.-E. (1997). Self-definition and mental health during adolescence and young adulthood. In J. Schulenberg, J. M. Maggs, & K. Hurrelmann (Eds.), *Health risks and developmental transitions during adolescence* (pp. 395–419). Cambridge, England: Cambridge University Press.

Ogbu, J. U. (1978). *Minority education and caste: The American system in cross-cultural perspective.* New York: Academic Press.

Ogbu, J. U. (1985). A cultural ecology of competence among inner-city blacks. In M. B. Spencer, G. K. Krookins, & W. R. Allen (Eds.), *Beginnings: The social and affective development of black children* (pp. 45–66). Hillsdale, NJ: Lawrence Erlbaum Associates.

Ogbu, J. U. (1989). Cultural boundaries and minority youth orientation toward work preparation. In D. Stern & D. Eichorn (Eds.), *Adolescence and work: Influences of social structure, labor markets, and culture* (pp. 101–140). Hillsdale, NJ: Lawrence Erlbaum Associates.

Owens, T. J. (1993). Accentuate the positive—and the negative: Rethinking the use of self-esteem, self-deprecation, and self-confidence. *Social Psychology Quarterly, 56,* 288–299.

Owens, T. J. (1994). Two dimensions of self-esteem: Reciprocal effects of positive self-worth and self-deprecation on adolescent problems. *American Sociological Review, 59,* 391–407.

Parker, J. G., Rubin, K. H., Price, J. M., & DeRosier, M. E. (1995). Peer relationships, child development, and adjustment: A developmental psychopathology perspective. In D. Cicchetti & D. J. Cohen (Eds.), *Developmental psychopathology. Risk, disorder, and adaptation* (Vol. 2, pp. 96–161) New York: Wiley.

Pearlin, L. I., & McCall, M. E. (1990). Occupational stress and marital support: A description of microprocesses. In J. Eckenrode & S. Gore (Eds.), *Stress between work and family* (pp. 39–60). New York: Plenum.

Pearlin, L. I., Menaghan, E. G., Lieberman, M. A., & Mullan, J. T. (1981). The stress process. *Journal of Health and Social Behavior, 22,* 337–356.

Peskin, H., & Livson, N. (1972). Pre- and postpubertal personality and adult psychologic functioning. *Seminars in Psychology, 4,* 343–355.

Petersen, A. C., Leffert, C. N., Graham, B., Alwin, J., & Ding, S. (1997). Promoting mental health during the transition to adolescence. In J. Schulenberg, J. M. Maggs, & K. Hurrelmann (Eds.), *Health risks and developmental transitions during adolescence* (pp. 471–497). Cambridge, England: Cambridge University Press.

Petersen, A. C., Sargiani, P., & Kennedy, R. (1991). Adolescent depression: Why more girls? *Journal of Youth and Adolescence, 20,* 247–272.

Petersen, A. C., & Taylor, B. (1980). The biological approach to adolescence: Biological change and psychological adaptation. In J. Adelson (Ed.), *Handbook of adolescent psychology* (pp. 117–158). New York: Wiley.

Peterson, J. L., & Zill, N. (1986). Marital disruption, parent–child relationships, and behavior problems in children. *Journal of Marriage and the Family, 48,* 295–307.

Phillips, S., & Sandstrom, K. (1990). Parental attitudes toward "youthwork." *Youth and Society, 22,* 160–183.

Piotrkowski, C. S., & Crits-Christoph, P. (1981). Women's jobs and family adjustment. *Journal of Family Issues, 2,* 126–147.

Quinn, R. P., & Staines, G. L. (1979). *The 1977 quality of employment survey.* Ann Arbor, MI: Survey Research Center, Institute for Social Research.

Quinton, D., Rutter, M., & Liddle, C. (1984). Institutional rearing, parenting difficulties and marital support. *Psychological Medicine, 14,* 107–124.

Rathunde, K., & Csikszentmihalyi, M. (1991). Adolescent happiness and family interaction. In K. Pillemer & K. McCartney (Eds.), *Parent–child relations throughout life* (pp. 143–162). Hillsdale, NJ: Lawrence Erlbaum Associates.

Reitzes, D. C., & Mutran, E. J. (1994). Multiple roles and identities: Factors influencing self-esteem among middle-aged working men and women. *Social Psychology Quarterly, 57,* 313–325.

Richards, M. H., & Larson, R. (1989). The life space of socialization of the self: Sex differences in the young adolescent. *Journal of Youth and Adolescence, 18,* 617–626.

Robins, L. N. (1966). *Deviant children grown up: A sociological and psychiatric study of sociopathic personality.* Baltimore, MD: Williams & Wilkins.

Robinson, N. S., & Garber, J. (1995). Social support and psychopathology across the life span. In D. Cicchetti & D. J. Cohen (Eds.), *Developmental psychopathology. Risk, disorder, and adaptation* (Vol. 2, pp. 162–209). New York: Wiley.

Rook, K. S. (1992). Detrimental aspects of social relationships: Taking stock of an emerging literature. In H. O. F. Veiel & U. Baumann (Eds.), *The meaning and measurement of social support* (pp. 157–170). New York: Hemisphere.

Rosenberg, M. (1965). *Society and the adolescent self-image.* Princeton, NJ: Princeton University Press.

Rosenberg, M. (1979). *Conceiving the self.* New York: Basic Books.

Rosenberg, M., & McCullough, B. C. (1981). Mattering: Inferred significance and mental health among adolescents. In R. G. Simmons (Ed.), *Research in community and mental health: A research annual* (Vol. 2, pp. 163–182). Greenwich, CT: JAI Press.

Ross, C. E., & Mirowsky, J. (1987, August). *A structural social psychology of depression: Control and support.* Paper presented at the American Sociological Association, Chicago, IL.

Rowlinson, R. T., & Felner, R. D. (1988). Major life events, hassles, and adaptation in adolescence: Confounding in the conceptualization and measurement of life stress and adjustment revisited. *Journal of Personality and Social Psychology, 55*, 432–444.

Rutter, M. (1979). Protective factors in children's response to stress and disadvantage. In M. W. Kent & J. E. Rolf (Eds.), *Primary prevention of psychopathology: Vol. 3. Social competence in children* (Vol. 3, pp. 49–74). Hanover, NH: University Press of New England.

Rutter, M. (1983). Stress, coping, and development: Some issues and some questions. In N. Garmezy & M. Rutter (Eds.), *Stress, coping, and development in children* (pp. 1–41). New York: McGraw-Hill.

Rutter, M. (1985). Resilience in the face of adversity: Protective factors and resistance to psychiatric disorder. *British Journal of Psychiatry, 147*, 598–611.

Rutter, M. (1990). Psychosocial resilience and protective mechanisms. In J. Rolf, A. S. Masten, D. Cicchetti, K. H. Neuchterlein, & S. Weintraub (Eds.), *Risk and protective factors in the development of psychopathology* (pp. 181–214). New York: Cambridge University Press.

Rutter, M., & Quinton, D. (1984). Long-term follow-up of women institutionalized in childhood: Factors promoting good functioning in adult life. *British Journal of Developmental Psychology, 2*, 191–204.

Savin-Williams, R. C., & Berndt, T. J. (1990). Friendship and peer relations. In S. S. Feldman & G. R. Elliott (Eds.), *At the threshold: The developing adolescent* (pp. 277–307). Cambridge, MA: Harvard University Press.

Schuster, T. L., Kessler, R. C., & Aseltine, R. H. (1990). Supportive interactions, negative interactions, and depressed mood. *American Journal of Community Psychology, 18*, 423–438.

Shanahan, M. J., & Mortimer, J. T. (1996). Understanding the positive consequences of psychosocial stress. In B. Markovsky, M. Lovaglia, & R. Simon (Eds.), *Advances in group processes* (Vol. 13, pp. 189–209). Greenwich, CT: JAI Press.

Silbereisen, R. K., & Walper, S. (1988). A person-process-context approach. In M. Rutter (Ed.), *Studies of psychosocial risk: The power of longitudinal data* (pp. 96–113). New York: Cambridge University Press.

Simmons, R. G. (1978). Blacks and high self-esteem: A puzzle. *Social Psychology, 42*, 54–57.

Simmons, R. G. (in press). Comfort with the self. In T. J. Owens, S. Stryker, & N. Goodman (Eds.), *Extending self-esteem theory and research: Sociological and psychological currents.* New York: Cambridge University Press.

Simmons, R. G., & Blyth, D. A. (1987). *Moving into adolescence: The impact of pubertal change and school context.* New York: Aldine.

Simmons, R. G., Blyth, D. A., Van Cleave, E. F., & Bush, D. M. (1979). Entry into early adolescence: The impact of school structure, puberty, and early dating on self-esteem. *American Sociological Review*, *44*, 948–967.

Simmons, R. G., Brown, L., Bush, D. M., & Blyth, D. A. (1978). Self-esteem and achievement of black and white adolescents. *Social Problems*, *26*, 86–96.

Simmons, R. G., Burgeson, R., Carlton-Ford, S., & Blyth, D. A. (1987). The impact of cumulative change in early adolescence. *Child Development*, *8*, 1220–1234.

Simmons, R. G., Burgeson, R., & Reef, M. J. (1988). Cumulative change at entry to adolescence. In *Minnesota symposium on child psychology: Development during the transition to adolescence* (Vol. 21, pp. 123–150). Hillsdale, NJ: Lawrence Erlbaum Associates.

Simmons, R. G., Rosenberg, M., & Rosenberg, F. (1973). Disturbance in the self-image at adolescence. *American Sociological Review*, *39*, 553–568.

Simon, R. W. (1997). The meanings individuals attach to role identities and their implications for mental health. *Journal of Health and Social Behavior*, *38*, 256–274.

Smetana, J. G., Yau, J., Restrepo, A., & Braeges, J. L. (1991). Conflict and adaptation in adolescence: Adolescent–parent conflict. In M. E. Colton & S. Gore (Eds.), *Adolescent stress: Causes and consequences* (pp. 43–65). New York: Aldine de Gruyter.

Spencer, M. B., Dornbusch, S. M., & Mont-Reynaud, R. (1990). Challenges in studying minority youth. In S. S. Feldman & G. R. Elliott (Eds.), *At the threshold: The developing adolescent* (pp. 123–146). Cambridge, MA: Harvard University Press.

Steinberg, L. D. (1987). Recent research on the family at adolescence: The extent and nature of sex differences. *Journal of Youth and Adolescence*, *16*, 191–197.

Steinberg, L. D. (1990). Autonomy, conflict and harmony in the family relationship. In S. S. Feldman & G. R. Elliott (Eds.), *At the threshold: The developing adolescent* (pp. 255–276). Cambridge, MA: Harvard University Press.

Steinberg, L. D., & Avenevoli, S. (1998). Disengagement from school and problem behavior in adolescence: A developmental-contextual analysis of the influences of family and part-time work. In R. Jessor (Ed.), *New perspectives on adolescent risk behavior* (pp. 392–424). Cambridge, England: Cambridge University Press.

Steinberg, L. D., & Cauffman, E. (1995). The impact of employment on adolescent development. *Annals of Child Development*, *11*, 131–166.

Steinberg, L. D., & Silverberg, S. B. (1986). The vicissitudes of autonomy in early adolescence. *Child Development*, *20*, 1017–1025.

Stryker, S. (1980). *Symbolic interaction: A social structural version*. Menlo Park, CA: Benjamin/Cummings.

Suls, J. (1989). Self-awareness and self-identity in adolescence. In J. Worell & F. Danner (Eds.), *The adolescent as decision-maker: Applications to development and education* (pp. 144–180). San Diego, CA: Academic Press.

Thoits, P. A. (1983). Dimensions of life events that influence psychological distress: An evaluation and synthesis of the literature. In H. B. Kaplan (Ed.), *Psychosocial stress: Trends in theory and research* (pp. 33–103). New York: Academic Press.

Thoits, P. A. (1985). Social support and psychological well-being: Theoretical possibilities. In I. B. Sarason & B. R. Sarason (Eds.), *Social support: Theory, research, and applications* (pp. 51–72). Dordrecht: Marinus Nijhoff.

Thoits, P. A. (1991). On merging identity theory and stress research. *Social Psychology Quarterly*, *54*, 101–112.

Thoits, P. A. (1995). Stress, coping, and social support processes: Where are we? What next? *Journal of Health and Social Behavior* (Special Issue), pp. 53–79.

Thomas, M. E., & Hughes, M. (1986). The continuing significance of race: A study of race, class, and quality of life in America, 1972–1985. *American Sociological Review*, *51*, 830–841.

Tyszkowa, M. (1993). Adolescents' relationships with grandparents: Characteristics and developmental transformations. In S. Jackson & H. Rodriguez-Tome (Eds.), *Adolescence and its social worlds* (pp. 121–143). Hillsdale, NJ: Lawrence Erlbaum Associates.

U.S. Bureau of the Census. Data users service division. (1982). *Census of population and housing, 1980: Summary tape file 3. Technical documentation.* Washington, DC: U.S. Government Printing Office.

Valverde, S. A. (1987). A comparative study of Hispanic high school dropouts and graduates: Why do some leave school early and some finish? *Education and Urban Society, 19,* 320–329.

Wacquant, L. J. D. (1992). The social logic of boxing in black Chicago: Toward a sociology of pugilism. *Sociology of Sport, 9,* 221–254.

Wallace, J. M., & Williams, D. R. (1997). Religion and adolescent health-compromising behavior. In J. Schulenberg, J. M. Maggs, & K. Hurrelmann (Eds.), *Health risks and developmental transitions during adolescence* (pp. 444–468). Cambridge, England: Cambridge University Press.

Ware, J. E., Johnston, S. A., Davies-Avery, A., & Brook, R. H. (1979). Current HIS mental health battery (r-1987/3-Hew) Appendix E. In J. E. Ware, S. A. Davies-Avery, & R. H. Brook (Eds.), *Conceptualization and measurement of health for adults in the health insurance study: Vol. III. Mental health* (pp. 94–105). Santa Monica, CA: Rand Corporation.

Weiss, R. S. (1990). Bringing work stress home. In J. Eckenrode & S. Gore (Eds.), *Stress between work and family* (pp. 17–38). New York: Plenum.

Werner, E. E. (1987). Vulnerability and resiliency in children at risk for delinquency: A longitudinal study from birth to young adulthood. In J. D. Burchard & S. N. Burchard (Eds.), *Prevention of delinquency* (pp. 16–43). Beverly Hills, CA: Sage.

Werner, E. E., & Smith, R. S. (1982). *Vulnerable but invincible: A study of resilient children.* New York: McGraw-Hill.

Wethington, E., & Kessler, R. C. (1986). Perceived support, received support, and adjustment to stressful life events. *Journal of Health and Social Behavior, 27,* 78–89.

Wheaton, B. (1990). Where work and family meet: Stress across social roles. In J. Eckenrode & S. Gore (Eds.), *Stress between work and family* (pp. 153–174). New York: Plenum.

Windle, M. (1992). A longitudinal study of stress buffering for adolescent problem behaviors. *Developmental Psychology, 28,* 522–530.

Youniss, J., & Smollar, J. (1985). *Adolescent relations with mothers, fathers, and friends.* Chicago, IL: University of Chicago Press.

APPENDIX A

Measures

SOCIAL BACKGROUND

Socioeconomic Status (Household income and parental education are standardized and combined; when available, the educational attainment of both parents is averaged.)

How much schooling did you complete?

Less than high school graduation (1) to Ph.D. or professional degree (8)

What was your total household income in 1987 before taxes?

Under $5,000 (1) to $100,000 or more (13)

CHANGE IN FAMILY

Family composition

Who do you live with?

(1) Mother and father (by birth or adoption)
(2) Mother (by birth or adoption)
(3) Mother and stepfather
(4) Father (by birth or adoption)
(5) Father and stepmother
(6) Part of the time with each parent
(7) Another relative
(8) A foster parent
(9) Other, please specify _____

Father's Employment Status

Have you ever been to his place of work?

Does not apply because he does not work (1) No (2) Yes

FAMILY COMFORT

Parent–child Relationship (The same set of questions are asked for both mother and father)

How close do you feel to him/her?

Extremely close (4) to Not close at all (1)

When you are faced with personal concerns and decisions, do you talk them over with him/her?

Never (1) to Often (4)

How often does he/she talk over important decisions that he/she has to make with you?

Never (1) to Often (4)

How often does he/she listen to your side of an argument?

Never (1) to Often (4)

How often do you do things with him/her that you enjoy?

Never (1) to Often (4)

Comfort with mother: Cronbach's alpha Grade 9 = .829, Grade 10 = .842, Grade 11 = .846.
Comfort with father: Cronbach's alpha Grade 9 = .832, Grade 10 = .853, Grade 11 = .848.

PEER COMFORT

Peer support

When things get rough, do you have a friend (or friends) who you can really talk to, someone you can turn to for support and understanding?

Yes, I am very sure I do (1) to No, I don't (4)

SCHOOL COMFORT

Teacher support

How often are your teachers willing to listen to your problems and help find solutions?

Never (1) to Almost always (5)

Time pressures

How often is there time pressure when you do your school work?
Never (1) to Almost always (5)

WORK COMFORT

Supervisor support (Cronbach's alpha Grade 9 = .560, Grade 10 = .659, Grade 11 = .691)

How often is your supervisor willing to listen to your problems and help find solutions?
Almost always (1) to Never (5)

How close do you feel to your supervisor?
Extremely close (1) to Not close at all (4)

Support from coworker

How close do you feel to your *best* friend at work?
Extremely close (1) to Not close at all (4)

Work satisfaction

How satisfied are you with your job as a whole?
Extremely satisfied (1) to Extremely dissatisfied (6)

Work stress (Cronbach's alpha Grade 9 = .640, Grade 10 = .696, Grade 11 = .674)

How often is there time pressure on your job?
Never (1) to Almost always (5)

How often are you exposed to excessive heat, cold, or noise at work?
Never (1) to Almost always (5)

I have too much work to do everything well.
Not at all true (1) to Very true (4)

My job requires that I work very hard.
Not at all true (1) to Very true (4)

I feel drained of my energy when I get off work.
Not at all true (1) to Very true (4)

Work is interesting/boring

How often do you feel bored at work or that time is dragging?

Almost never (1) to Always (5)

ADJUSTMENT MEASURES

Achievement:

Grade Point Average

What is your grade point *average* so far this year? (Circle ONE LETTER)

A A– B+ B B– C+ C C– D+ D D– F

Mental Health Indicators (Standardized lambda coefficients are reported in parentheses for Grades 9 and 10, respectively):

Depressive affect

Each statement below was rated on a 5-point scale from (1) *none of the time* to (5) *all of the time.*

During the past month, how much of the time:

Have you been under any strain, stress, or pressure? (.470; .488)

Have you felt downhearted or blue? (.700; .726)

Have you been moody or brooded about things? (.616; .640)

Have you felt depressed? (.826; .857)

Have you been in low or very low spirits? (.788; .818)

Well-being

Each statement below was rated on a 5-point scale from (1) *none of the time* to (5) *all of the time.*

During the past month, how much of the time:

Have you felt that the future looks hopeful and promising? (.434; .481)

Have you generally enjoyed the things you do? (.511; .566)

Have you felt calm and peaceful? (.584; .646)

Have you felt cheerful, lighthearted? (.519; .575)

Self-efficacy

Each of the following statements was rated on a 4-point scale from *strongly disagree* (1) to *strongly agree* (4):

There is really no way I can solve some of the problems I have. (.501; .503)

Sometimes I feel that I'm being pushed around in life. (.356; .357)

I have little control over the things that happen to me. (.430; .431)

I can do just about anything I really set my mind to do. (.212; .212)

What happens to me in the future mostly depends on me. (.106; .106)

I mostly feel helpless in dealing with the problems of life. (.487; .488)

There is little I can do to change many of the important things in my life. (.405; .406)

Self-esteem

Each of the following statements was rated on a 4-point scale from *strongly disagree* (1) to *strongly agree* (4)

I feel I have a number of good qualities. (.278; .312)

I take a positive attitude toward myself. (.506; .567)

On the whole, I am satisfied with myself. (.469; .526)

Self-derogation

Each of the following statements was rated on a 4-point scale from *strongly disagree* (1) to *strongly agree* (4):

I certainly feel useless at times. (.499; .543)

I feel I do not have much to be proud of. (.423; .461)

I wish I could have more respect for myself. (.522; .568)

At times I think I am no good at all. (.608; .662)

Dichotomous Specification
of Comfort Measures
and Tenth-Grade Frequencies

FAMILY COMFORT

Perceived Comfort with Mother

How close do you feel to her?		%	
discomfort (0)	not close at all	6.2	
	fairly close	19.8	= 26.0
comfort (1)	quite close	34.9	
	extremely close	39.0	= 73.9

When you are faced with personal concerns and decisions, do you talk them over with her?

discomfort (0)	never	12.5	
	rarely	24.0	= 36.5
comfort (1)	sometimes	40.0	
	often	23.6	= 63.6

How often does she talk over important decisions that she has to make with you?

discomfort (0)	never	10.1	
	rarely	27.4	= 37.5
comfort (1)	sometimes	41.4	
	often	21.1	= 62.5

How often does she listen to your side of an argument?			
discomfort (0)	never	8.1	
	rarely	20.7	= 28.8
comfort (1)	sometimes	40.5	
	often	30.7	= 71.2

How often do you do things with her that you enjoy?

discomfort (0)	never	4.3	
	rarely	22.5	= 26.8
comfort (1)	sometimes	51.3	
	often	21.9	= 73.2

Cutoffs noted were established to specify presence or absence of comfort, and the items were summed. The additive parental comfort construct was recoded to follow a fairly strict definition of comfort: The adolescent must be comfortable on four or more items to be considered comfortable in their relationships with mothers. The same method is used to create the father comfort construct.

Comfort with mother:	Value	f	%	
discomfort (0)	0	79	8.6	
	1	79	8.6	
	2	97	10.6	
	3	121	13.2	= 41.0
comfort (1)	4	182	19.8	
	5	360	39.2	= 59.0
	Total	918	100.0	

Perceived Comfort with Father[1]

How close do you feel to him?

discomfort (0)	not close at all	17.0	
	fairly close	31.0	= 48.0
comfort (1)	quite close	29.6	
	extremely close	22.4	= 52.0

When you are faced with personal concerns and decisions, do you talk them over with him?

discomfort (0)	never	27.9	
	rarely	34.4	= 62.3
comfort (1)	sometimes	29.5	
	often	8.2	= 37.7

How often does he talk over important decisions that he has to make with you?

discomfort (0)	never	24.1	
	rarely	33.4	= 57.5

---

[1]The measure of comfort with fathers considers adolescents' relationships with fathers who currently live with them and fathers who do not but are in contact with the adolescents.

| comfort (1) | sometimes | 32.3 | |
| | often | 10.2 | = 42.5 |

How often does he listen to your side of an argument?

discomfort (0)	never	17.1	
	rarely	23.1	= 40.2
comfort (1)	sometimes	34.0	
	often	25.8	= 59.8

How often do you do things with him that you enjoy?

discomfort (0)	never	11.8	
	rarely	25.8	= 37.6
comfort (1)	sometimes	44.1	
	often	18.3	= 62.4

Comfort with father:	Value	f	%	
discomfort (0)	0	160	18.5	
	1	130	15.0	
	2	128	14.8	
	3	146	16.9	= 65.2
comfort (1)	4	131	15.1	
	5	170	19.7	= 34.8
	Total	865	100.0	

Family Discomfort

A single indicator was created that combines the adolescent's relationships with both mother and father. That is, Adolescents who have distant or noncommunicative relationships with both parents are considered uncomfortable.

	Frequency	%
comfortable	615	64.4
uncomfortable	340	35.6
	955	100.0

PEER COMFORT

Peer support

When things get rough, do you have a friend who you can really talk to, someone you can turn to for support and understanding?

		%	
discomfort (0)	No, I don't.	8.1	
	I'm not sure.	4.6	
	I'm fairly sure I do.	26.6	= 39.3

comfort (1)   I'm very sure I do.   60.7   = 60.7
                               $N = 853$

SCHOOL COMFORT

Teacher support

How often are your teachers willing to listen to your problems and help
find solutions?

		%	
discomfort (0)	never	2.0	
	rarely	13.4	
	sometimes	28.5	= 43.8
comfort (1)	often	34.4	
	almost always	21.8	= 56.2
	$N = 949$		

Time pressure

How often is there time pressure when you do your school work?

		%	
comfort (1)	never	3.0	
	rarely	22.7	
	sometimes	40.1	= 65.8
discomfort (0)	often	26.1	
	almost always	8.1	= 34.2
	$N = 949$		

WORK COMFORT

Supervisor support

How often is your supervisor willing to listen to your problems and
help find solutions?

		%	
discomfort (0)	almost never	3.9	
	rarely	10.7	
	sometimes	18.7	= 33.2
comfort (1)	often	32.0	
	always	34.7	= 66.7
	$N = 337$		

How close do you feel to your supervisor?

discomfort (0)	not close at all	21.1	
	fairly close	40.4	= 61.4

comfort (1)	quite close	25.5	
	extremely close	13.1	= 38.6
	$N = 337$		

Comfort with supervisor:	Value	f	%	
discomfort (0)	0	97	28.8	
	1	124	37.1	= 65.9
comfort (1)	2	115	34.1	= 34.1
	$N = 337$			

Support from coworker

How close do you feel to your best friend at work?

		%	
discomfort (0)	not close at all	13.4	
	fairly close	40.7	= 54.0
comfort (1)	quite close	27.9	
	extremely close	18.1	= 46.0
	$N = 337$		

Work satisfaction

How satisfied are you with your job as a whole?

		%	
discomfort (0)	extremely dissatisfied	2.2	
	very dissatisfied	3.6	
	somewhat dissatisfied	8.7	= 14.6
comfort (1)	somewhat satisfied	45.1	
	very satisfied	29.8	
	extremely satisfied	10.5	= 85.3
	$N = 446$		

Work stress

How often are you under time pressure?

		%	
comfort (1)	never	18.0	
	rarely	27.9	
	sometimes	27.3	= 73.2
discomfort (0)	often	18.0	
	almost always	8.9	= 26.9
	$N = 451$		

How often are you exposed to excessive heat, cold, or noise at work?

| comfort (1) | never | 20.4 |
| | rarely | 18.8 |

	sometimes	19.5	= 58.8
discomfort (0)	often	19.7	
	almost always	21.5	= 41.2
	$N = 451$		

I have too much work to do everything well.

comfort (1)	not true	47.5	
	little true	33.3	= 80.8
discomfort (0)	somewhat true	14.4	
	very true	4.7	= 19.1
	$N = 444$		

My job requires that I work very hard.

comfort (1)	not true	19.0	
	little true	32.7	= 51.7
discomfort (0)	somewhat true	29.1	
	very true	19.2	= 48.3
	$N = 447$		

I feel drained of my energy when I get off work.

comfort (1)	not true	25.3	
	little true	33.1	= 58.4
discomfort (0)	somewhat true	26.4	
	very true	15.2	= 41.6
	$N = 447$		

Cutoffs noted were established to specify presence or absence of comfort, and work stress items were summed. The construct was recoded so that employed adolescents reporting high levels of stress (i.e., discomfort on four or more of the five items) are considered uncomfortable on the measure of work stress.

Work stress construct:	Value	f	%	
discomfort (0)	0	22	5.0	
	1	37	8.4	= 13.4
	2	73	16.6	
	3	97	22.0	
comfort (1)	4	108	24.5	
	5	103	23.4	= 86.5
	Total	440	100.0	

Work is interesting/boring

How often do you feel bored at work, or that time is dragging?

		%	
comfort (1)	never	6.0	
	rarely	23.3	
	sometimes	41.7	= 71.0
discomfort (0)	often	21.5	
	almost always	7.5	= 29.0
	$N = 451$		

Author Index

Subject Index